3· 2525 90398 9356

BERLIN-PECK MEMORIAL LIBRARY

SO-BAS-596

Wild
Tulips

BERLIN-PECK
MEMORIAL LIBRARY
BERLIN, CT 06037

Beth Bruno

BERLIN-PECK
MEMORIAL LIBRARY
BERLIN, CT 06037

649.1

BRuno

12.95

2/5/03

Wild Tulips
By Beth Bruno
Copyright © 2001

■TRI-STATE LITHO
■ ■ BOOK AND PUBLICATION PRINTING
71-81 Tenbroeck Ave.
Kingston, NY 12401

All rights reserved by the author including the
right of reproduction in whole or in part in any
form

Library of Congress Control Number: 2001130128
ISBN: 0-9708430-0-3

Disclaimer: Information and suggestions provided in
this book, unless otherwise noted, are based on the
author's personal and professional experiences and are
not intended as prescriptions for the reader. The author
advises readers who have questions or concerns about
their child's development or school adjustment to
consult personally with teachers, physicians or other
specialists for guidance.

Send comments about Wild Tulips to: Beth Bruno
Email address: ladybeth81@hotmail.com

Dedicated to:

My grandmother, who taught me to listen with my heart.

My father, who taught me that solutions to problems evolve, just like people do.

My mother, who taught me to delight in the unexpected.

My husband and children, who taught me that leaning on each other makes us stronger.

Acknowledgments

The cultivation of ideas for print takes many hearts and minds, not just the author's. I am fortunate that so many friends, family members and literary professionals have been willing to contribute their encouragement, stories and expertise to help me grow *Wild Tulips.*

Thank you: Bill and Rose Bauman, father and step-mother; Geoff and Nikki Bruno, Terry Nelson and Cindy Battaglia, son, daughter and stepdaughters – each of whom contributed personal stories; Nikki and Gordon Bruno, Roberta Buland, Jan Kozlowski and William Rodarmor, editors; Bob and Jeanne Danielson, Gena Hamilton, Bobbie and Dick Searles, Jim and Ceil Spero, Gail Figliola and Kay Browne, friends and contributors; breakfast club pals, Dorothy Barnhart, Audrey Lefkowitz, Sharon Burch and Ellen Ornato, and finally the membership of the Connecticut Authors and Publishers Association(CAPA) — for expertise about the ins and outs of publishing and constant encouragement to dig the furrows, plant the seeds, weed out pests and reap the harvest.

Contents

Introduction
Germination

"Please stay off my train," begged the conductor, staring at my protruding belly.

"Don't be silly, Max," I countered, stepping off the platform onto the train. "You will be a hero!"

Max and I had become friends over the three years I commuted to graduate school in New York to study psychology. We liked telling each other stories about the loveable characters in our lives. Lately, though, Max was preoccupied with my advancing pregnancy. I glanced at his vest pocket where he kept a small book about delivering babies. Behind it, wrapped up tight, was a pair of sterile scissors.

"Just my luck, you'll go into labor on my shift," he groaned.

"Stop worrying, Max. My last class is this Friday, and I'm not due until next week. Two more days and you're home free. Come on now and help me find a seat. I did my breathing exercises while standing in the aisle last week, but nobody budged. So I sat in one of the bathroom sinks all the way to New York!"

Max strode purposefully into the next car. He put his hand on the first shoulder he reached and said gruffly, "Sir, give this woman your seat, please."

The man looked up from his newspaper, clearly annoyed, but he caught sight of me and got up quickly. A dark look from Max stifled any complaints.

I thanked the gentleman profusely and eased into the seat. Two more days and I could kiss this cattle car goodbye.

"Thanks, Max. Thanks for everything. Talking with you is the only thing I'll miss about this train."

"Uh-huh," he blushed. "See you tomorrow, you hear?"

Max lucked out. Friday's commute passed without incident. After returning from New York in the afternoon, I finished writing my last term paper, stuffed it into a manila envelope, addressed it and put it by the front door as a reminder to mail it. Done with classes at last! I breathed a sigh of relief, looking ahead to three free months before starting my clinical internship. I could finally give all of my attention to the new baby.

"You can come out now, little one," I whispered. "Everything is ready for you."

I dove energetically into cleaning the bathroom. Maternal nesting is certainly a remarkable and powerful phenomenon. I had never been a fastidious housekeeper, but once I was finished with our floors, I swear that you could eat off them. I insisted on hiring someone to clean the house from top to bottom; then, after she left, I cleaned everything again.

Later that afternoon, while crouched on all fours scrubbing the linoleum, I felt a gush of warm water puddle around my knees. A few seconds later my abdomen cramped tightly and released.

"Oh my God, I'm in labor! Where's Gordon? This isn't supposed to be happening yet! Oh my God!" I scooted on a bath towel into the kitchen and called the obstetrician, who told me what to do. How could he be so calm? I was having a baby!

Gordon left his office right away and drove me to the hospital. Eleven hours later, we were parents. From the moment I saw our infant son, my priorities changed forever. This squalling child had, by some miracle, been placed in my hands — in our hands. All else paled by comparison.

I was completely entranced by Geoffrey's every move — fascinated by his moods and the elemental ways he communicated with me. The unfolding of this tiny person's life provided structure and meaning to my life in ways nothing else ever had.

Admittedly, I felt ignorant and nervous, too. Before we went home, the hospital nurses had instructed me about breastfeeding and shown Gordon and me how to bathe a newborn; but after that we were on our own. I expected that my husband, already the father of two, would be an old hand with babies, but he had worked two jobs and attended graduate school full-time during his daughters' early years, so his ex-wife was the expert there. Honestly, I think he was as nervous as I was, although I doubt he would admit it.

Most of what I knew about babies I had read in books. Growing up, I was the baby in the family — the youngest of five — and I rarely babysat as a teenager. One time I agreed to take care of my dentist's six-month-old daughter for the afternoon. I remember laying her on the bed to change her, and while I was searching in the bureau for dry pants, I heard a thud behind me. I whirled around, my heart in my mouth. The baby had rolled right off the bed onto the floor! I scooped up the whimpering child and looked her over for bumps and bruises. She wasn't hurt, just startled, but she sure gave me a scare. I had no idea babies could move so quickly.

As it turns out, my professions — teacher and school psychologist — have been especially valuable to me as a parent. Working in schools, clinics and hospitals has afforded me countless opportunities to observe and interact with parents and children of all ages, thereby enriching my understanding of child development through their eyes as well as my own. Whenever I succeed professionally at helping a child or family remove an obstacle to learning or adjustment, I experience the same thrill I feel as a mother when I help solve a knotty problem at home.

I have written this book for my children Geoff and Nikki; for my stepchildren Terry and Cindy; for my husband Gordon; for my extended family; and for you and your families. The knowledge and personal discoveries contained in these pages come mostly from what parents and children have taught me during ordinary events that occur in households and schools everywhere. My hope is that insights from my stories will resonate with yours and perhaps lead to resolutions of some of the challenges you face.

I know intuitively that you and I — regardless of differences in race, culture, religion or circumstances — have a common bond. We deeply love our children and strive to do what is best for them; at the same time we strive for personal growth, to do what is best for ourselves.

Each life, like each flower in a garden, has a beauty all its own.

Chapter One
Seedlings

Every spring, milkweed pods burst open, releasing dozens of tiny white parachutes — each carrying a single seed — aloft into the breeze. One by one the seeds come to rest. Only those that fall on fertile ground take root and grow to adulthood, provided they find adequate nourishment, sunlight and protection from the elements.

Human seeds also carry the potential for growth, a miracle that begins with fertilization. Unlike plants, however, babies can only survive to reproductive age with many years of succor from nourishing adults. Vulnerable but resilient, each baby interacts with its social and physical environment, experience that lays the groundwork for the development of mind, body and spirit.

Whether from plant or animal origins, every seed contains traits inherited from previous generations, traits that may persist, die away, mutate or combine to form new ones in the crucible of life.

Plenty of Thyme

My grandmother listened with her heart. She was a tall, serene, silver-haired woman who wore granny glasses over twinkling, soft eyes. Somehow baggy cotton dresses were becoming on her as she tended her lush tropical flowerbeds in central Florida. We loved to visit and pore over old photograph albums together, while she recounted detailed family adventures about each picture.

She raised six boys, Grandma did, among them my Dad, now an octogenarian with the same twinkling, soft eyes. Those boys adored her. They wrote and visited often and took care of her until her last breath at age one hundred. I'm convinced that she reached the century mark mostly because of the affection, attention and profound respect that surrounded her.

No one could spend fifteen minutes with Grandma without becoming a little bit wiser. She told me about a time my Dad was stumped by a physics problem. He was anxious and worried about his inability to solve it, especially the night before an exam. Grandma told him to go to bed and sleep on it. "Your mind will work it out," she assured him. Sure enough, the next morning he solved the problem easily and aced the exam, partly because he had let his mind relax and organize itself and partly because he had had such a good night's sleep. Mostly, Grandma's confidence in him gave him confidence in himself.

I have watched Dad repeat those same steps over the years. After he works for weeks on a chemical research problem or on a tough puzzle like the Rubik's Cube, he lets sleep work its special magic and, voilà, the solution becomes clear.

Children were especially drawn to my grandmother. When she and Grandpa visited us, kids came from around the neighborhood to share their thoughts with her, just to see her face light up with interest as she responded to each one. She always made each of us feel important and special.

At bedtime Grandma sat on the edge of my bed and told me stories about her childhood.

"When I was twenty years old," she said, "I saved some money and bought my first bicycle."

"Didn't you have a car, Grandma?" I asked.

"Goodness, no, child, there were no cars in aught-three (1903), just dirt streets and horse-drawn carriages."

"No cars? Gee! Did you ride a horse to school?"

"No, our horse dragged the plow and worked on the farm during the week and pulled us to town in the carriage on weekends. My friends and I walked two miles to school every day, uphill both ways."

"Is that really true, Grandma?"

"Why certainly, Bethie," she replied with a wink and a smile. "Uphill both ways."

My children were two and five years old when Grandma died. They met her a few times but only vaguely remember her. I often show them the old family photograph albums to recount stories about their great-uncles, great-aunts and great-grandparents. In so doing, I keep Grandma's wit and wisdom alive for all of us.

Braidwood Brilliant

Whispers of "genius" followed him everywhere, although no one ever called him that to his face. Bill Bauman, my dad, knew he was different as a child. He skipped first and third grades and eventually graduated from high school with his older brother George, who had started out three years ahead of him.

Boys from the local quarry, who had been held back in school, were not impressed. "Think you're so smart?" they sneered, as they ambushed him and shoved him face-first into the snow. They never really hurt him; they just kept him mighty scared — and humble, too.

After graduating from Hawken, a private preparatory school in Cleveland, fifteen-year-old Bill was too young to gain admission to college, so he took shorthand and typing at the public high school. Under the tutelage of an art instructor there, he also learned the intricacies of woodcarving, pewter-molding, and batiking cloth.

The following year, as a college freshman, he attended the Case School of Applied Science before winning a full scholarship to Yale University, where he completed an undergraduate degree and a Ph.D. in chemistry.

Bill married his longtime sweetheart, Janet Kenny. They settled and raised five children in Midland, Michigan, headquarters of the Dow Chemical Company, his employer until retirement forty years later.

Chemical research stretched Bill's inquisitive mind to the fullest. His early experiments centered on the development of ion exchange resins used to soften and purify water supplies. He developed Dowex 50®, a cation exchange resin of unique and reproducible structure. He proposed the use of Dowex 50® as a universal tool for the recovery and purification of inorganic and organic cations, from plutonium to amino acids. Soon Dow added Dowex 1®, a comparable anion exchange resin, to the tool kit to extend the utility of ion exchange to all ions. Bill has published many papers defining the properties of Dowex 50® and Dowex 1®, leading to their use in research laboratories around the world.

In addition to making new ion exchange resins, Bill found ways to use ion exchange to extract specific minerals from brine, a dense salt and mineral solution found underground in several locations around the world. Dow Chemical located in Midland because of the rich brine fields there. When brine is run through an ion exchange resin selective for a specific mineral such as magnesium, calcium, or lithium, the "captured" mineral can then be made available commercially. Lithium, for example, is an important element used in the production of batteries. Bill has developed a process of recovering magnesium from seawater using ion exchange.

Now retired but never inactive, Bill continues to develop new ideas for selectively extracting minerals from brine. His basement lab, not quite as fancy as the one at Dow, contains an old electric frying pan, a microwave oven, a small electronic scale, and various resins and crystals, which he uses to test out his hypotheses. At age eighty-five, he's more inventive than ever, and now that he has retired, he owns the patents himself! He recently sold two patents to an international chemical company, which is investing millions of dollars in his remarkable, cost-effective lithium extraction process.

Dad only recently told me about the bullies who had terrorized him for being so smart. I am immensely relieved that they never actually hurt him. His inventive, playful mind kept my siblings and me entertained and constantly curious through the years. Dad knew he was different; it's lucky for all of us that he was happy to stay that way.

Scent of Jasmine

When I was little, my curiosity was forever getting me into trouble. One time, while visiting at a neighbor's house, I noticed several colored glass bottles lined up by the bathroom sink. They were exquisite bottles in different shapes and sizes, one pearly green, another sapphire, and still another with a delicate, tapered cap like a church spire. Unable to suppress my curiosity, I picked up a tiny, luminescent pink bottle by its thick oblong top. Just as I brought it over my lap, the bottom part fell and amber liquid splashed on me, its sweet, floral scent filling the air.

Puzzled, I looked at the glass stopper in my hand. I had never seen a non–twist-off cap before. As I retrieved the empty bottle, thankfully unbroken, and gently replaced the stopper, I felt my heart begin to pound.

"This must be expensive perfume," I thought, "like the ones from Paris that cost $50 an ounce."

I was too scared to admit I had spilled it. I put the bottle back on the vanity, raced home, took off my skirt, and threw it down the laundry chute, hoping my dilemma would evaporate with the perfume.

When the neighbor later called my mother and told her what had happened, Mom confronted me. I denied any wrongdoing. Mom insisted I go get the clothes I had been wearing, so I ran downstairs, grabbed the skirt, took it upstairs to my parents' bedroom, and doused it with some of my mother's cologne. I then took the skirt to Mom to prove it was her perfume I had spilled on my clothes, not the neighbor's.

Mom did not accuse me of lying. She just listened and believed me — or so I thought. I didn't hear another word about it until some thirty years later when I asked Dad if he remembered the incident. He did. He told me that he and Mom had talked it over and decided to tell the neighbor, within earshot of me, that I had denied spilling it. (I don't remember hearing them say that.) They felt that they should back me up, rather than embarrass me more than I had already embarrassed myself. They wanted guilt to teach me a lesson.

It certainly did. I felt terrible about it for years, and I still do. In retrospect, I wish my parents had asked me to replace the perfume, either by working hard to earn the money, or by doing chores for the neighbor until she was satisfied I had paid her back. With no solution, I was left with the shame and no way to redeem myself.

Intense childhood experiences like these shape our adult values. As a mother, I've worked hard to instill the value of honesty in my children. I want them to admit their mistakes and make amends for them, if possible.

My husband applied similar principles as a high school principal. He devised imaginative punishments that taught students about personal responsibility. Vandalism, for example, was punishable by janitor duty. This policy resulted in the cleanest school windows and bathrooms in the state! His students learned important lessons when held accountable for their actions.

How I wish I could have stuffed the perfume back into that bottle. To this day, when I go by that neighbor's house, I feel a twinge of guilt for lying to her. Some good came of it, I suppose. My cowardly behavior probably served as an object lesson to her children for years to come. Little does she know that my insatiable curiosity survived intact. But now when it gets me into trouble, I admit it!

Monk's Beard

We drove from Michigan to Kentucky together — my dad, my twenty-two-year-old brother Bill and I — when I was seventeen. It must have been fall because I can still picture leaves skittering across the road in swirling eddies of red, orange and yellow. A few miles from our destination we rounded a sharp curve and came upon a horrible accident. A sports car had slid off the road and crashed into the rocks, turning it into a mangled heap of metal. No one could have survived that crash. I wondered why the wreckage was still there — why no one had hauled it away. There were no signs of anyone around. It rattled me, as if it were a bad omen.

Stunned, we continued our journey deep in thought. We arrived in Bardstown late in the afternoon and followed our directions to the Gethsemane Abbey. The road to the monastery wound through rolling farmland, freshly tilled after the summer harvest. We parked across from the main building; Bill collected his bags from the trunk; and we walked through the front gates into a small courtyard. The bearded man who greeted us looked just like I had imagined a monk would look. He was dressed in a brown hooded robe and wore a wooden crucifix around his neck.

"Welcome to Gethsemane, Bill," he began. "I am Brother John. How was your trip?"

After we introduced ourselves and exchanged a few pleasantries, Brother John told us about life at the monastery. The monks follow the rule of St. Benedict by praying together as a community seven times a day. Their prayers, called the divine office, include the Psalms, Torah, Prophets, Bible and other religious texts. They celebrate Mass every day, as well.

"We lead a quiet, contemplative life here," Brother John said, "praying for our community, for the Church and for all humankind."

The monastery is financially self-sustaining; the brothers grow much of their own produce and bring in money by making cheese, fruitcakes and bourbon fudge, for sale by mail-order.

While Brother John was talking with us I noticed a second monk approaching. He stood nearby and nodded to acknowledge us but did not speak.

"Brother Timothy will show you to your quarters, Bill, whenever you are ready."

"I'm ready now," Bill said in a soft, steady voice. He was smiling and seemed eager to get started. He hugged Dad and me, assuring us that he would write letters home, and then walked inside with his escort. In disbelief, I watched him walk away.

Brother John extended a warm invitation, which Dad and I accepted, to attend Mass at the monastery chapel before heading back.

The chapel was beautiful in its simplicity. The ceilings, altar and pews were hewn of dark wood. Votive candles flickered beside the altar, which was draped in white linen. Soft lights illuminated the crucifix that hung over the altar, and a gold chalice rested on the linen cloth. Before Mass began, we heard low, chanting voices approaching the chapel. A procession of monks appeared, walking two by two with their hands folded, chanting Latin prayers in unison, letting their voices drop at the end of a phrase before taking a breath and returning to the higher note for the next phrase.

"Dominus vobiscum," they intoned.

"Et cum spiritu tuo," we replied.

I looked for Bill, but he was not among them. The rise and fall of the monks' voices, their muffled footsteps and the rustling of their robes soothed me. I felt safe and completely at peace in this profoundly spiritual place. I began to understand why Bill was drawn to this quiet oasis in the hills.

Even so, I was totally opposed to his decision to become a Trappist monk. How could he give up marriage and raising a family? Why was this brilliant man — an artist, mathematician, poet and student of the classics — shutting himself away from the world? For what? His life had barely begun. He could not serve humanity by shielding himself from it.

During the ride home I told Dad how I felt. He listened sympathetically but maintained his neutrality. Before marrying my mother, a devout Catholic, he had signed a pledge that any children they had would be raised in the Catholic faith. He did not participate in our religious education but occasionally attended Mass with us. I still know very little about his religious beliefs; he left our religious education up to my mother and the Church. We attended public schools and learned about many different religious traditions from teachers and friends.

After we returned home, I wrote to Bill almost every day. My letters contained all the reasons I thought he was making a huge mistake and why he should come home and lead a full life. I was determined to convince him that any life outside the monastery walls was better than life could ever be inside them.

He sent an occasional letter to the family and just one letter directly to me. His letters to the family described his daily routine and the simplicity and beauty of his life at Gethsemane.

In his letter to me he wrote, "Beth, try to think of the universe as an atom or group of atoms. Electrons orbit the nucleus of the atom and each electron follows its own distinct path. The orbit of each electron contributes equally to the stability of the whole. If one electron is pushed or pulled out of its orbit, the atom becomes unstable and can even break apart completely.

"I think about people in the same way. Every person moves in a unique orbit, too. Right now mine has brought me here to the monastery. My prayers are just as important as your flute playing or Dad's inventions or Mom's delicious pies. The different paths we take contribute equally to the universe and keep it stable and intact."

I respected Bill's choice after that. I still didn't like it much, and I missed him terribly. But I understood his explanation and appreciated its message. In fact, it made me feel stronger and more courageous myself. If what he said was true, it meant that I could choose my own path, too, and that whatever I chose would make a unique and special contribution to the world. I even found myself feeling happy for him.

Less than a year later I answered an unexpected phone call from Bill.

"Hi, Beth," he said. "I'm downtown at the bus station. Will you come and pick me up?"

He had decided to come home. Not because his beliefs had changed — they had not. He came home because he was allergic to pollen from the fields and dust kicked up while sweeping the chapel and sleeping quarters. His sinuses were so badly stuffed up he could barely breathe, let alone pray. Nothing he tried brought relief. He had no choice, he said, but to leave.

Bill accepted what happened as God's will. God had called him to the monastic life; it had not worked out; so God encouraged Bill to serve Him in other ways. My brother's faith helped him accept this disappointment and embrace the future without lamenting the past.

I interpreted these events differently. In my opinion, Bill's allergies and return home had nothing to do with God's will. He decided to leave of his own free will. But then that is the view from my orbit, not his. He and I will each find our own path.

Mock Orange

"May I take your order from the bar?"

"A Shirley Temple, please," I replied in my most sophisticated voice, hoping I wouldn't have to show the fake ID card I had borrowed from an upperclassman.

"And you, sir?"

"Scotch on the rocks, please."

The waiter returned with our drinks. "Our specials tonight are ..."

Distracted, I ordered something for dinner and reached for the tall bubbly liquid, topped with a maraschino cherry.

"Here's to decadence," I laughed. We clinked glasses. I sipped hesitantly, expecting unfamiliar flavors, but the drink tasted surprisingly sweet, like a carbonated fruit punch.

During dinner I ordered two more Shirley Temples, becoming more talkative and silly with each one. When we rose to leave I felt so lightheaded, I clung to my date's arm to steady myself.

"You punchy dame," he jibed. "You're teetering! What's wrong with you?"

"Nothing's wrong," I insisted. "Watch this." I let go of his arm and tried to walk an imaginary line, heel to toe, heel to toe, but I nearly toppled over. "Whoa," I giggled. "Guess I can't hold my liquor very well."

"What liquor?" He shook his head. "There's no liquor in a Shirley Temple!"

"There isn't?"

Flushed with embarrassment, I sobered up fast, appalled that the power of suggestion had literally intoxicated me.

In medicine this power is called the "placebo effect," long recognized as a powerful ingredient in the healing process. As Dr. Walter A. Brown reports in the January 1998 edition of *Scientific American*, research has shown that 30 to 40 percent of people diagnosed with depression, chronic pain, high blood pressure or asthma benefit from taking a placebo. Brown states, "A patient's expectation of improvement is crucial." For example, when research participants were told that a nonalcoholic drink contained alcohol, they often felt and acted intoxicated. Some even showed physiological signs of intoxication, just as I had!

One study, Brown says, conducted by the U.S. Office of Technology Assessments, suggests that "only 20 percent of modern medical remedies in common use have been scientifically proven to be effective. It is not that these treatments do not offer benefits: most of them do. But the benefits may come from the placebo effect, in which the very act of undergoing treatment helps the patient recover."

Despite negative connotations associated with placebos — such as the notion that one's symptoms are all in the mind — their impact is real and should, therefore, be embraced by medical practitioners. "The healing environment itself can be a powerful antidote for illness," Brown writes. A thorough physical examination, attention from nurses and other medical staff, explanations of symptoms and assurance of a favorable prognosis reduce anxiety, which frequently leads to symptom reduction.

When doctors take the time to find out what a patient thinks will help, it often does. A diagnosis, prescription (even for an over-the-counter remedy) and a prognosis that defines the course of the ailment gives the patient a sense of control over it. When several treatment options are available, patients do better when they make the choice themselves, after the doctor has provided sufficient information about possible side effects and treatment outcomes.

Harnessing the placebo effect and using it to contribute to the healing process can help doctors and patients avoid common pitfalls, such as demanding and prescribing pills or procedures that have no intrinsic value for the condition being treated, such as prescribing antibiotics for colds. Alternative remedies such as massage, herbs and multivitamins belong in the treatment mix, too, not only for proven benefits, but also because consumers believe in their effectiveness.

When treating children, one of the pediatrician's most powerful allies is the primary caregiver. That person is likely to know when a child's symptoms become serious enough to require treatment, as well as what treatments have been effective in the past. From the caregiver's perspective, confidence and trust in the physician might help prevent illness, too.

The healing power of the mind is one of modern medicine's most powerful allies in the art of healing the body.

Black-Eyed Susans

The dark staircase wound steeply to the fifth floor. Not that the darkness mattered to Mr. Stibbs — he had been blind since birth.

People often asked him why he lived in a fifth floor walk-up. "To keep in shape," was always his reply. Which was the truth. He needed to keep his body and mind healthy to make up for his lack of sight.

To stay abreast of the news and to enjoy books unavailable on tape or in Braille, Mr. Stibbs hired college students to read to him. Later that afternoon, a new reader was coming to his apartment, a coed from the University of California in Berkeley. He was looking forward to her company, although he had grown weary of the same old questions and comments from newcomers. "What's it like to be blind?" "How does the cane work?" "How can you read with your fingertips?" "That's amazing!"

Usually after students' curiosity about his condition was satisfied, they started arriving late or not at all, and he had to find another reader. He kept hiring students, because their hourly rates were low and the university could always supply new help quickly.

Mr. Stibbs tidied up the kitchen and tested the new chair he had just finished making out of an old pile of Braille books. He was proud of his creative "recycling" projects, mostly chairs, shelf supports, and assorted small tables he had crafted from the large, heavy-paged volumes. Visitors marveled at their sturdiness and unique design.

No sooner had he finished vacuuming the living room floor than the buzzer sounded. The intercom confirmed the arrival of the coed, so he pressed the button to let her in. She arrived at the landing, a bit out of breath from the climb.

They exchanged introductions and settled down to read and listen to each other. Their conversation centered on the content of the articles and became a lively exchange. The planned hour turned into two before either of them realized it. She apologized for taking so much of his time, arranged their next appointment and left.

"She didn't ask a single question about my condition," he thought. "I think she genuinely enjoyed herself."

They became fast friends. She often read her college essays to Mr. Stibbs to solicit his opinions and suggestions before handing them in. He made her a paper chair, which she and her friends liked so much he made them two more. "The next ones," she insisted, "I'll make my friends pay for!"

The school year flew by. In May, the coed informed Mr. Stibbs that she was leaving, not only for the summer, but also for a year of study abroad. He invited her to go out to lunch downtown to celebrate her new adventure and their friendship.

On the appointed day, she took the arm he offered, using his cane in the other hand, as they negotiated the winding staircase and stepped onto the sidewalk. The café where they were having lunch was just a few blocks down Shattuck Avenue. They stood at the curb chatting while waiting for the light to change. When she saw the signal change, she tugged slightly on Mr. Stibbs' arm as she stepped off the curb to cross. He quickly drew her back, as a car came speeding around a curve from the left. Mr. Stibbs had heard it easily and knew they weren't safe yet, while her dependency on the signal light had nearly caused her serious harm.

Over lunch, the questions tumbled forth. "How did you know that car was coming? When did you go blind? How did you learn Braille?"

He answered her questions eagerly and proudly, because he knew that in her eyes, his disability had become an ability.

I was that lucky coed, and I will never forget my afternoons with Mr. Stibbs. I like to think that he will never forget them either.

Passion Blossoms

Thirty years ago, as an undergraduate psychology major, I wrote a paper entitled "Measurement of Emotional Development." People gradually mature emotionally as well as intellectually, I asserted, so we should devise a way to measure one's EQ (Emotional Quotient) just as we have measured the IQ (Intelligence Quotient) for many years. I thought the idea of an EQ was very clever. The professor agreed, but was not impressed with my literature review on the subject. He gave the paper a "C."

The idea continued to intrigue me. About a year later I approached the subject from a slightly different angle. Emotional maturation and the development of creativity are closely linked, I wrote, because people with high self-esteem are more likely to take creative risks than people who are insecure. Since creativity and ego strength are both measurable traits, it should be possible to quantify the degree of correlation between the two. Again I introduced the idea of the EQ (Emotional Quotient), comparing it this time to the CQ (Creativity Quotient). My extensive documentation and suggested research model impressed the professor, who not only gave me an "A," but also asked me to present the ideas to the class. Following a lively discussion with fellow students, I returned to my studies feeling happy and duly recognized.

I went on to complete master's degrees in education and psychology and have been a student of human development ever since — as a teacher, psychotherapist, school psychologist and parent. Frankly, it never again occurred to me to research my EQ - IQ - CQ hypotheses.

Then, a few months ago, I came across two newspaper articles about the book *Emotional Intelligence*, by Daniel Goleman, Ph.D. (Bantam 1997). Goleman poses and answers the following question: "What factors are at play when people of high IQ flounder and those of modest IQ do surprisingly well?" He asserts that, "The difference quite often lies in the abilities called here *emotional intelligence*, which include self-control, zeal and persistence, and the ability to motivate oneself. These skills can be taught to children, giving them a better chance to use whatever intellectual potential the genetic lottery may have given them."

This groundbreaking book goes on to describe the neurological underpinnings of one's emotions and the gradual process people undergo to learn to modulate impulses, read the feelings of others and handle relationships more smoothly. Low emotional intelligence can lead to broken marriages, aggression, poor health, criminal behavior, disastrous career choices and teen pregnancy.

At the Nueva Learning Center in Hillsborough, California, students can focus on understanding their emotional lives in a course called "Self Science." Goleman writes, "The subject is feelings — your own and those that erupt in relationships. The topic, by its very nature, demands that teachers and students focus on the emotional fabric of a child's life — a focus that is determinedly ignored in almost every other classroom in America." Karen Stone McCown, the developer of the Self Science Curriculum, writes, "Learning doesn't take place in isolation from kids' feelings. Being emotionally literate is as important for learning as instruction in math and reading."

The implications of this book for schooling are far-reaching. Current emphasis on reading, writing, and arithmetic is well placed; however, schools must also attend to the equally important skills children need to become socially and emotionally literate. By studying the arts, humanities, conflict resolution, and ethics, for example, children learn about aesthetics, motivation, compassion and fairness.

To teach academics alone is to teach to half of a person's potential. A brilliant boor, for example, will most likely alienate others. The intellect and the emotions are as inseparable as the two intertwined genetic strands that form the DNA helix. One cannot thrive without the other. The approach we take when educating our children should reflect this fundamental truth.

Cupid's Dart

I have always been a pretty casual person, the wash-and-wear type, you might say. Getting ready for work or a night on the town takes me ten minutes, tops. I jump into the shower, throw on some clothes, run a comb through my wet hair and let it dry on the way out. Not one to wear much makeup, I apply moisturizing lipstick without a mirror while in the car or on foot. What takes other people so long to get ready? "Come on," I say, "let's go!"

The man I was dating several years ago especially liked my style. Although more polished than I, Gordon could be disarmingly spontaneous. One summer night after dinner at a local hotel, we left the restaurant along a hallway next to the indoor pool. Suddenly, without warning, he leaped into the water — suit, shoes and all! I nearly collapsed with laughter as he came up spouting water like a surfacing whale. He was irresistible.

Oh, what the hell! I teetered on the edge, spread my arms out to the side and fell in backward with a huge splash.

Ours was a long-distance relationship. Gordon lived in New York, I in Boston. One weekend he invited me to a black-tie affair at the opening of an art gallery in New York. I decided to surprise him with supreme, beautifully coifed elegance. On Saturday morning at a Newbury Street salon, the stylist swept my long hair into an updo of glorious curls. I had purchased a deep red sheath gown with matching shoes, perfect for the lasting impression I hoped to make.

Ordinarily, on such a hot September day, I would have wrapped my hair in a scarf and driven my MG convertible to the city with the top down. But not this time. I wanted to protect every curl.

I arrived around four o'clock, boiling hot and soggy, but when I checked my hair in the mirror, it still looked great. Relieved, I retrieved my garment bag and locked the car. The doorman buzzed me into the apartment building where I rode the elevator to the twelfth floor. I couldn't wait to see my honey's expression.

He greeted me with a warm hug and long kiss. Then he stepped back to take a look.

"It's great to see you," he said. "You look as gorgeous as ever. But what happened to your hair? Did you drive here with the top down?"

So much for elegance. We got married three months later.

Chapter Two
Nutrients

Nutrients that support healthy physical development are relatively easy to identify and provide. We instinctively feed, shelter and protect our young from bodily harm.

Not so obvious, but equally vital, are the nutrients essential for emotional and cognitive health. We know that children need loving touch and engaging interaction with parents and other caregivers, and they need safe learning environments that are conducive to exploration and experimentation. We are less sure, however, what methods produce optimal results. Is it better to teach a skill directly or to let a child imitate or discover it? Should we intervene when children disagree or let them resolve disputes on their own? How do children overcome fear? What will help every child achieve his or her personal best?

Since babies do not come with instructions and each baby is different, we have to learn from them what enhances their development and what interferes with it. Our babies teach us while we teach them!

Chatterboxes

The brain of a baby is still forming long after the child has left the womb — not merely growing bigger, as toes and livers and arms do, but forming the microscopic connections responsible for feeling, learning, and remembering.
— "How to Build a Baby's Brain," by Sharon Begley, Special Edition of Newsweek, Spring/Summer 1997.

Scientists are learning that the stimulation of experiences after birth, rather than something innate, determines the actual wiring of the human brain. Peek-a-boo, play with blocks or beads, touch, early music lessons and thousands of other interactions strengthen synaptic connections (the wiring) and lead to permanent cognitive, motor, language, social and emotional learning patterns.

The infant brain forms neural connections at an astounding rate, writes Begley. In the second half of the first year of life, for example, the prefrontal cortex, which is the seat of planning and logic, forms synapses so fast that it consumes twice as much energy as an adult brain. In the first months of life, the number of synapses increases about twenty-fold.

Research on language acquisition has shown how "neuroplastic" an infant's brain is, plasticity that diminishes with age as neural connections form and become more specialized. The size and complexity of a toddler's speech, for example, depends on the amount and quality of language he hears from those who interact with him most. Only live language, not television, boosts vocabulary and sentence complexity. "Language has to be used in relation to ongoing events, or it's just noise," Begley reports. Add cuddling, smiling, singing and other loving behavior between parent and child and learning enhancement is even more pronounced.

The downside of the infant brain's great plasticity is its vulnerability to trauma. In some abused children, portions of the brain have been shown to be 20 to 30 percent smaller than normal, and synaptic development is reduced. Trauma can also scramble neurotransmitter signals, which causes children exposed to chronic and unpredictable stress to suffer deficits in their ability to learn.

This information about infant brain development has profound implications for the education of our children. During the first three years of life, the rate of brain development reaches its peak, yet we do not usually begin formal education until age 4 or 5, after huge amounts of learning have already taken place. Ironically, the vast majority of our best-educated mothers and fathers work outside the home and leave their infants and young children in the care of modestly educated, minimum-wage-earning adults, who may know little about optimum conditions for mental, social and emotional human development.

Research suggests that our most highly motivated and loving infant educators, namely parents and early childhood specialists, should be interacting with and educating our young. Makeshift arrangements, low wages and indifferent care (or worse) lead to abysmal developmental outcomes for many U.S. children. I think we should make it a national priority to increase salaries of the early childhood labor force, support family-friendly, licensed childcare centers and fund intensive parent-education programs.

Think of the newborn baby's brain as an unwritten symphony. Little by little, through interaction with the human and physical environment, notes cluster into phrases, rhythms and harmony. Whether each symphony makes music or noise depends on the richness and quality of those interactions, which only the most enlightened caregivers can provide.

Baby's Breath

Until I was twenty-nine years old, I could go out my front door anytime I wanted. Then came the "blessed event," all eight pounds and four ounces of him. We were ecstatic.

Ecstatic, that is, until the first morning we ran out of milk. Baby was asleep; hubby was at work; and I wanted cereal. So I bundled up Baby and headed for the nearest Wawa. Naturally my bundle was wailing by this time, and I was beginning to wish I had settled for eggs and ham. Such a hassle for a little milk! Goodbye, freedom.

That's right. Spontaneity was history. Twenty-four hours a day, seven days a week, one of us had to stay home. Unless, of course, we could find a babysitter. So with telephone in hand, confident but naïve, we entered the babysitter market.

Friends steered us down the teen aisle. We even tried an occasional preteen, only to discover that anyone under twelve will raid the refrigerator, talk nonstop on the phone and ignore the kids. After all, they are only kids themselves. Thirteen- and fourteen-year-olds are perfect. Then they hit high school and buy date books, which they promptly fill to overflowing until they graduate.

One year we hit the babysitter jackpot. A house was sold in our neighborhood to a family with four children, the oldest a senior in high school. She resented leaving her old friends, so she decided not to bother making new ones until she went to college. She was usually available nights and weekends to baby-sit. What's more, she loved our kids. A year of freedom was ours.

But when I decided to go back to work part-time, we had to shop the adult babysitter market. Not lucky enough to have relatives close by, and reluctant to send our kids to a daycare center, we decided to advertise for someone to come to the house.

The first woman we hired was the grandmother of five. She

had unruly, white hair and no teeth, but our children thought she was absolutely beautiful. Several peaceful days passed. Then one evening a neighbor, who lived across the street, told me she found our four-year-old in her son's tree house that afternoon — unwatched. Grandma was home playing patty-cake with the baby, I guess. Farewell, grandma.

The next woman came highly recommended, with her three-year-old son in tow. A perfect arrangement, I thought. The boys could play together while she attended to the baby. One winter night, as she prepared to leave, she helped her son into his parka, tied the hood and put on his mittens. As we stood by the front door chatting, her son waited patiently for awhile, but started getting hot, so undid his hood and took off his mittens. When she noticed this, she grabbed him by the hair and started screaming at him! So long, lady.

We still suffer babysitter-from-hell flashbacks of the woman we decided not to hire after she told us she always carried a pistol in her purse to protect the children she watched. Then there was the teenage boy who locked the doors and fell into such a deep sleep we had to call from next door and let the phone ring for twenty minutes to wake him — and it was only 11 p.m.!

So, just remember, all you teenagers and young couples out there who romanticize parenthood. Think twice and be prepared. Because when you say, "Hello, baby," you simultaneously say, "Goodbye, freedom!"

Silent Verbena

Listen to the language of silence. It speaks volumes between uncommunicative spouses.

"Honey, what would you like for dinner tonight?"

"Mumble, mumble."

Silence: He's so annoying. We get home from work; I offer to make dinner; and he falls asleep. Well, I'm hungry now!

At 8:00 p.m., honey wakes up.

"Hey, I'm famished. Where's my dinner?"

"Gosh, when I asked you what you wanted two hours ago, you never answered. I figured you weren't hungry, so I fixed myself something."

"You did what?"

***

It can even discipline kids.

"Cathy, don't forget to clean your room."

"Groan."

Silence: I'm sick of nagging her about that pigpen. I wonder how long she can stand it.

Three days later: "Has anyone seen my math book?"

"The last time I saw it, it was in your room."

"How am I supposed to find it in there? The place is a mess!"

Silence: It's about time!

The next day: "I got an 'F' on my math test."

"That's terrible, Cathy. Math is your favorite subject. How did that happen?"

"I didn't clean my room."

Silence: I think she got the message.

Later that night. "Wow, look at this place. It looks fantastic! Did you find your math book?"

"Yup," proudly, "and my volleyball, Frisbee, best jeans, favorite lipstick and two dollars I thought I lost!"

"Hey, that's great, honey."

***

It's absolutely symphonic with teenagers.

"Dad, can I borrow the car?"

"Sure, Jason. It needs gas, though."

"O.K."

Slam. Later that night: Rrrrrrring! "Dad, this is Jason. I ran out of gas."

"Uh-huh."

Silence: Why does he have to learn everything the hard way? He's just like I was at his age.

"Dad?"

BERLIN-PECK
MEMORIAL LIBRARY
BERLIN, CT 06037

"Uh-huh."

"Did you hear me? I ran out of gas!"

"Uh-huh."
"Can you come and get me?"

"In what?"

"Oh yeah, I have the car. Never mind, I'll handle it."

***

I don't think most people realize how powerful silence can be. Or how respectful. When you ask someone a question and wait for a response, your silence says, *"I want to know what you think. I value your opinion. Without your input, this conversation can't go on."*

Watch children relax under the golden touch of silence. It takes time for a child to formulate her thoughts. She is often unsure of herself and might say, "I don't know," just to give herself time to think. When she does that, try saying, "OK I'll get back to you later on that one." Silence: *She looks so relieved!* Often, before you get back to her, she will come to you, eager to share her ideas.

Intimacy thrives on silence. Sharing deeply held emotions can leave one feeling vulnerable and bare, so much so that some people cry, even when expressing profound joy. A natural impulse is to babble reassurances, when instead, a soft, holding silence breathes acceptance into the moment and lets it be.

Mistletoe

The best gift I ever received came from my husband and children, written on a piece of paper, tucked into an envelope and hidden among the boughs of our Christmas tree.

A CHRISTMAS GIFT RESOLUTION FOR LADY BETH

WHEREAS Lady Beth's disdain for the domestic art of dishwashing is known far and wide, owing to years of exploitation in a male-dominated household; and,

WHEREAS such disdain has become exacerbated since even in her seasoned adulthood as mother, wife, and almost full-time professional worker, she remains involuntarily attached to this oh-so-dismal chore; and,

WHEREAS her two children and husband, Kathryn Nicole, Geoffrey Alexander and Gordon August Bruno, together find themselves feeling especially appreciative of their meals and the countless other things Lady Beth does for them day in and day out; and,

WHEREAS in that same spirit of appreciation the three aforementioned characters met and considered numerous and sundry ways to express their gratitude to their closest relative during this joyous Christmas season,

NOW THEREFORE BE IT RESOLVED that, effective at twelve o'clock midnight on the thirty-first of December, in the year of our Lord Nineteen hundred and eighty-three, our terrific Lady Beth is hereby and forthwith relieved of any and all dishwashing for a period of time not to exceed one full calendar year, or twelve o'clock midnight on the thirty-first of December, Nineteen hundred and eighty-four;

AND BE IT FURTHER RESOLVED that, in pursuit of active schedules of work and play, often quite different one from the other, the aforementioned characters all vow that they will spare Lady

Beth from even the slightest quibbling or argument as to whose turn it is to do what or who might be doing more than the other in the daily act of implementing said gift. Such conversations, if they should be necessary at all, are to be conducted in private among the givers of the gift and not in the presence of the recipient.

SIGNED, PLEDGED, SEALED, NOTARIZED AND OTHERWISE MADE LEGAL AND BINDING ON THIS CHRISTMAS EVE DAY, DECEMBER 24, 1983.

> WITH LOVE,
> Kathryn Nicole Bruno, Daughter
> Geoffrey Alexander Bruno, Son
> Gordon A. Bruno, Husband
> (All Signed)

At the end of 1984, without so much as a whisper of protest, my three "characters" renewed their pledge indefinitely. Upon retirement, Gordon promises he'll do the laundry, too!

Mums and Poppies

Dear Readers:

Take it from my brother and me. It isn't easy raising parents these days. First off, they're entirely too busy. Mom and Dad are the first to say, "You can't get better at anything if you don't practice." Well if that's true, how can they expect to be better parents if they're never home?

The time crunch gets so bad sometimes, we ask them to write us into their date books. They need to know we're serious about talking things over together without distractions. For awhile we arranged to have regular family meetings, which works out pretty well for planning vacations and negotiating allowances, but not so well when a crisis comes up. Whichever parent is around then has to step in and make a decision on the spot.

That's when our parents argue with each other about being consistent, because they don't want us to catch them contradicting each other. My brother and I think that's odd. We don't think alike; why should they? Look at it this way. They were never parents before we came along, so half the time they're just winging it anyway!

I remember when Mom grounded my brother for a week for getting a bad grade in English. Grounding him meant grounding her, too, because she had to stay home to make sure he stayed in his room and didn't use the phone. By the end of the week they were both miserable. Thank goodness she dropped that form of punishment before she used it on me!

Parents can be real busybodies. They seem to think that a history of changing diapers and bathing us gives them the right to know about everything we do or say.

"No, Dad, you can't walk into my room without knocking."

"No, Mom, you can't go through my stuff just to straighten it up."

We finally came up with a workable compromise. My brother and I agreed to clean our rooms once a week, without being told, and they agreed to stay out unless invited. After that, things were more considerate between us in lots of ways.

Teaching parents to listen better is tough. They have so much to say about how things were when they were our age, it's hard to get a word in edgewise. We appreciate their efforts to keep us from repeating their mistakes, but try as we might we only succeed in making new ones they never even thought of. Like the time I decided to turn the shower into a bathtub for my turtles. The stopped-up drain overflowed and created rain showers downstairs in the kitchen! Sometimes we have to learn things the hard way, just like they did.

To improve the balance of power, we like to treat our parents to a slice of humble pie every now and then. My brother crushes Mom at Ping-Pong, and we both run rings around them at computer games. After they've eaten their fill, they're pushovers!

Last but not least, we do set high expectations but we don't expect perfection. After all, they are new at parenting and need time to learn from their mistakes. Mom and Dad are still a bit rough around the edges, but so far they admit we're raising them pretty well.

Sincerely yours,
Nikki

Mountain Laurel

We taught our son to work hard and never give up. "You can accomplish anything you put your mind to," we said. As the old saying goes, "The difficult you do right away; the impossible takes a little more time."

Those were the thoughts flowing through Geoff's mind when his body screamed for relief halfway up a rock wall in the Berkshires. He clung to the crevices with every ounce of our belief in him, but his muscles couldn't respond. He had "hit the wall," with no choice but to allow fellow climbers to lower him to the bottom. He was crushed, his inner compass broken.

One by one his companions told him about times when each of them had run on empty and had had to seek and accept help. Every story helped him recognize his limitations as normal, not shameful. It was OK to fail, OK to learn from it and OK with his friends. During the next incident, he might well be the stronger one, there to help someone else.

This was the first of Geoff's many experiences with group esteem-building. He learned to relinquish control without punishing himself for it. Such mutual interdependence builds a form of self-esteem that leads to group cohesion and the tremendous power and potential for group problem solving, usually in situations that no individual can conquer alone.

Not that he gave up his belief in self-reliance. Never. He worked out every morning for the rest of the summer until he was able to climb that wall twice in one day! Even so, there was no going back to his old beliefs. He had found an even stronger belief in "other-reliance," a discovery that has contributed considerably to his effectiveness as a schoolteacher.

Important yet elusive, self-esteem is a trait that each of us needs in just the right amount. Too much produces conceit; too little produces self-doubt or anxiety. Just what is self-esteem, and how do we instill it in our children, in others and in ourselves?

Self-esteem is a belief in oneself, but not to the point of excessive pride or braggadocio. It is a calmness inside that lives there permanently, even when a person is under stress. I think of people who have strong self-esteem as resilient in good times and bad, because they believe in their ability to evaluate circumstances and survive whatever happens.

During dark moments, light can come from unexpected sources. When our daughter was five years old, my husband took a new job in another state, which meant upheaval caused by leaving close friends, finding a new job (for me), going to new schools (for the kids) and adjusting to a new town. My husband, son and I were grousing about the move one evening when our daughter demanded, "What's wrong with everybody? We're just moving!" Nothing like a cold bucketful of perspective from a kindergartner to bring us to our senses!

That sense of certainty can be elusive — solid one minute and shaky the next. There are days when I feel strong enough to tackle anything and do so; but on other days, the smallest disappointment sends me into full retreat. That's when I think about my son's experience of "hitting the wall" and realize how much I need to be able to lean on others when my own resources give out.

Giving self-esteem to others or acquiring it oneself is like walking a tightrope: trying to balance constructive criticism with high praise or a helping hand with urged independence. We cannot give or take the feedback in a vacuum because it comes from socializing with others, as reactions to what we do or say.

The balancing act is most difficult with children, whose inexperience makes them vulnerable to frequent falls. It is important to take the process of esteem-building slowly and quietly with children, giving them generous amounts of support, suggestions, encouragement, respect and love along the way. Let them experience the consequences of their actions, within the limits of safety, without choruses of "I told you so" when they make mistakes. And give them as many opportunities as possible to derive personal strength from times of interdependence among family members and friends.

Lonely Petunia

A one-way mirror covered one wall of the small room. Visitors sat behind it to observe developmental evaluations, which took place every Friday at the school for handicapped toddlers and preschool children where I worked.

Today's evaluation involved Henry, a three-year-old boy who had been uprooted as an infant, taken from an abusive mother and placed in foster care. The supervising family services agency referred him to us because his third foster mother, like the foster parents before her, could not make emotional contact with him. No one had heard him utter a single word; in fact, he scarcely made any sounds at all. When injured, he sometimes produced an eerie cry, a wail without tears.

On the afternoon of the evaluation, this slender boy with huge blue eyes and light blond hair took my hand limply and accompanied me to a small table in the middle of the room. He watched closely and accurately imitated my actions with blocks, crayons and other manipulatives used for cognitive assessment, but he did not vocalize or respond to sound. When the speech therapist called his name from another part of the room, he showed no reaction whatsoever. We began to wonder whether he could hear.

While other evaluators interacted with Henry, I left the room to watch from behind the one-way mirror. When his back was to the mirror and he was engrossed in play, I purposely slammed the door. Everyone in the room flinched except Henry.

Medical records indicated that brainstem testing had ruled out deafness, but anecdotal reports consistently raised questions about Henry's hearing. One neurologist had told Henry's caretakers that emotional trauma can severely impair a child's development. "Henry may never talk," he said.

Following the evaluation, Henry was enrolled in our preschool program, where he received speech therapy five days per week.

The first communication breakthrough occurred between Henry and the classroom teacher. She had brought in a basket of large, floppy hats, decorated with feathers and colorful ribbons. She engaged Henry in a simple game of trying on each hat, first on his head, then on hers. He smiled at her each time he saw a hat on her head. She reciprocated, with a big smile and exaggerated preening. Next she held up a large mirror so Henry could see himself in one of the hats. He took one look and burst out laughing, the first time any of us had ever heard him laugh. This game went on for weeks, much to the amusement of everyone in the school. He refused to play "hats" with anyone but his teacher.

Henry's class visited another preschool class each week to promote interaction between the special-needs children and more typically developing three-year-olds. Carol, the school cook, who absolutely adored the children, served them lunch family-style. Every day she greeted each of them by name, a greeting delivered with a warm smile and hug. Henry submitted to her hugs, but otherwise just watched her in his quiet, solemn way. She told us that the sadness she sensed under his reserve broke her heart.

At lunchtime during one of the weekly visits, the children were passing bowls of food around for their individual helpings, when Henry accidentally dropped the applesauce, half in his lap, the other half on the floor. Everyone looked at Henry; Henry stared at Carol. Moments into the silence, tears filled his eyes and began to spill down his cheeks. Carol went over, sat down on the floor beside him, and gathered him onto her lap. He nestled into her comforting arms and wept.

Everyone felt overjoyed, but no one more so than Carol' who could hardly wait to go home to tell her husband the news. She had been talking with him about Henry for weeks. Carol and Henry's attachment visibly strengthened after that, while in the background, she and her husband requested guardianship and began adoption proceedings. They wanted Henry to know they were making a permanent commitment to him, to be his parents forever. Shortly after the adoption papers went through, Henry started talking.

Dash of Sage

When you were a child, did the whole community seem to know you and delight in your accomplishments? That sense of neighborhood seems so rare now.

Our children know more than we did at their age. But they still need just as much adult guidance as ever, perhaps even more as their world becomes increasingly complex and fragmented. Families move more frequently; often both parents work long hours; fewer marriages survive; and children are exposed to mountains of verbal and visual information at an astounding rate. Yet, emotionally, a child is still a child. In these hectic times we need ways to reduce our isolation and talk with each other about effective parenting.

Lack of adult supervision can create dangerous situations for our young. Many high school and college student parties, for example, are awash in alcohol in defiance of home and school rules. Our children might act like they love their freedom, but they're unprepared for it, ultimately resentful and afraid to be so unprotected without defined and enforced limits from parents and other responsible adults. The young people who are prepared for freedom rather than thrown into it are proud to say, "No!"

The father of two teenage boys told me about his approach to setting reasonable limits for them.

"I am one of the few parents I know," he said, "who has risked the wrath of my sons by exercising parental control over who their friends are, what they do after school each day, what parties they are allowed to attend and what time they are expected home at night. I am up, awake and expect conversation when they arrive home at midnight (nineteen-year-old) and 11 p.m. (fifteen-year-old). I have made it clear what I expect from them and have created an environment in which they are not afraid to tell me 'stuff' that goes on in their world. They know I will come and get them wherever they are if they are uncomfortable with arrangements to get home.

"It really was not difficult. I am the parent, not a friend, and my sons are remarkably cooperative with the limits I have set. There was one shouting match when the older boy was fifteen or so, but that passed quickly when he realized that the scenarios I painted about what could happen at a party with no adults present, more often than not, did happen. I think kids want their parents to say 'no' when they ask permission to do something they are not sure they want to do. Parents just have to accept the mantle of parenthood and the responsibilities that entails. 'Fun' is a lot riskier for teens today."

My son told me about a college in New England where members of the hockey team were severely penalized for getting new recruits, mostly 18-year-old freshmen, drunk to the point of hospitalization during a celebration of their acceptance on the varsity team. Students at every college in the area were abuzz about this administrative action, because they were so surprised by it. They were also impressed and thankful that college officials had taken a stand against such dangerous consumption, even though it meant that the school's hockey team might win fewer games that season because of the suspensions imposed.

As a parent, I, too, was relieved that college officials, knowing full well that they had been minimizing such behavior for years, were at least willing to enforce statewide laws about liquor consumption by minors.

Children need adult guidance and supervision from birth through high school (and afterward). Parents and children alternately confront issues of autonomy throughout the years. In my estimation, the teen years are the trickiest ones in this transition from dependency to self-reliance, because teens tend to challenge adult authority at every turn and insist on chances to practice their independence. Parents, who recognize the potential dangers, find it hard to relinquish control and let their children learn from their mistakes.

But parents are not alone. We can seek advice from other parents, friends or counselors, especially during times when family communication breaks down. And, if our children or we get locked into patterns of defiance or excessive control, we need to swallow our pride and find help.

Hidden Truffles

Every person has a breaking point — a point at which the stress level is so high, it can no longer be suppressed or ignored. Some of the signs that you may be approaching yours include:

• Overreaction to minor incidents. Your nerves are so frayed that you fly into a rage and ground your son for a month for belching loudly at the dinner table.

• Underreaction to major incidents. The man applying shingles to your roof falls off the ladder and through the kitchen window. You glance over, tell him to clean up the mess, and continue reading the newspaper.

• Rapid gain or loss of weight. You have developed a love-hate relationship with food. You refuse dinner and then devour a gallon of ice cream and a package of Oreos that nauseate you to the point of vomiting. After that you are so disgusted with yourself, you eat nothing for two days.

• Constant worry and anxiety. Your daughter, age fifteen, will learn to drive next year. You get so worked up about the dangers she might face behind the wheel that you can't sleep, concentrate at work, relax, or follow a simple conversation. More worries piggyback on those.

• Excessive drug use, including alcohol, nicotine, and prescription and nonprescription drugs. You feel so lousy when you wake up every morning that you take something to make you feel better. You know such palliatives only work for a little while, but all you want right now is a few minutes' peace.

The main considerations here are severity and duration. Occasional extremes of behavior and mood affect us all. But when family and friends are telling you that it has gone on too long — and you know they are right even though you deny it — you need help. But from whom? Your fears about the choices sound worse than your problems:

A psychologist? No. Anybody with the word "psycho" in his title cannot be trusted.

A psychiatrist? No. Only crazy people who need drugs and locked hospital wards see them.

A social worker? No. They see people in groups, and I am not spilling my guts to a bunch of strangers.

A marriage and family counselor? No. The family has put up with enough already. No sense in dragging them into counseling, too.

A minister? A nutritionist? A biofeedback specialist? Alcoholics or Overeaters Anonymous? How on earth do I choose?

There are many well-trained, competent professionals and self-help groups available to support you through a crisis. Ask your family physician or trusted friends for recommendations. Then make an appointment and try to stifle assumptions about what will happen when you go.

Taking that first step into a mental health professional's office is a courageous step toward helping yourself. Talking with a therapist is a bit like talking with a stranger on a train, except this stranger has specialized training. Other than payment, you owe this person nothing. You are buying his or her expertise.

Anna's story is a case in point. The shock of infidelity had blown Anna's eight-year marriage apart. Fortunately, there were no children to suffer from the aftershocks. While patching her bruised ego together in short-term counseling, Anna enrolled in college and buried her insecurities under piles of reading assignments and term papers. She finished a four-year degree in business administration in time to catch a ride on the fast track in the whirlwind world of Internet start-up companies.

Flushed with pride in her achievements, yet beginning to feel lonely for male companionship, Anna decided to begin dating again. But time after time, if a man sought increased intimacy with her, she felt afraid and anxious, so much so that she immediately pushed him away. In conversation with her closest friend she admitted that she had never fully dealt with her feelings about her ex-husband's betrayal of trust. Her personal physician referred her to an experienced therapist.

There are no magical, instant cures from psychotherapy. Changing patterns of behavior and thought takes time, experimentation, open-mindedness, humility and courage. If the initial meeting goes well and leaves you feeling hopeful, give it a chance. If you leave feeling worse than when you walked in, and the approach offered makes no sense to you, interview other people before deciding whom you will hire to help you. Once you find someone whom you like and trust, the two of you will make treatment decisions together.

Resist letting irrational fears or personal pride stop you from getting professional help to work through an emotional crisis. Treatment for serious emotional conditions is as important as treatment for serious physical ones, because, left untreated, they not only can get worse, but also can be fatal. Your life is too precious to risk.

Chapter Three
Growth

Parents love to tell me stories about their children, invariably followed by the question, "Is that normal?"

"Our four-year-old daughter will only eat about ten different foods. She hates all vegetables except raw carrots. If two foods mingle on her plate, she won't touch either one. Is that normal?"

"After our divorce two years ago, our first-grader spends every other weekend in different households. To avoid punishment at home for acting up in school, he has begun lying about how his week went, hoping the teacher won't 'blow his cover' with one parent or the other. Is that normal?"

Normal development does not follow a predictable, steady path; it encompasses a broad range of behaviors and capabilities that appear in fits and starts from month to month and year to year throughout childhood, adolescence and adulthood.

No two people, even genetically identical twins, react to the world in the same way. Our minds and emotions sift through countless choices before taking action. Blended into the mix are conflicting messages from parents, friends, teachers, books and the media about right versus wrong. So we think things over, decide what is right for us at the time and move on.

Indian Paintbrush

Her taste in clothes ran to the theatrical. Summer or winter, no outfit was complete without sunglasses. One steamy August morning she came downstairs in plastic sandals, a short red-white-and-blue dress and four beaded necklaces, each one knotted at the bottom. She wore an oversized Mickey Mouse watch and bright red lipstick, penciled on slightly outside the lip line for that fuller look. Her hair was straight spun gold, worn in a Dutch-boy cut to frame her face.

Squat-heeled sandals clicked rhythmically on the oak floor as she strode into the kitchen pantry to find some cereal for breakfast. She was making another showstopper entrance, while I was doing my best not to stare. This morning's sunglasses had white frames with tiny red polka dots and dark black lenses, not the mirror kind, but opaque nonetheless. What a character! At the time she made this particular entrance, she had just turned three.

"I'm done with my cereal, Mom. Can Sadhana play today?"

"Let's give her a call," I replied. Sadhana's mom invited both of us to come over.

It was a perfect day for the girls to play outside while Barbara and I sipped iced tea on the porch. En route we bought some powdered paints for Sadhana's easel, which her dad had set up in their yard on a big plastic sheet to protect the grass.

After gleeful hugs, the girls inspected the bag of paints, put them by the front door, and scampered off to the swings for awhile. Barbara and I headed for the kitchen to steep hot tea before icing it down.

The girls' squeals moved from the side yard to the front porch and lingered there for some time. Our curiosity piqued, we walked to the front door, expecting to help mix the paints and check the easel's paper supply.

To our amazement, our enterprising daughters had turned on the garden hose and brought buckets of water onto the porch to mix the paints themselves. With brushes from the easel they were busily redecorating the front porch in brilliant swathes of red, yellow, and blue. Their laughter and broad smiles froze at the sight of us. No one moved.

I glanced warily at Barbara, waiting for the certain eruption that never came. She turned away and quietly disappeared into the house, ran up the stairs, and returned with her camera. She took several pictures of our paint-spattered, mischievous elves, grinning proudly at their handiwork. Naturally we had to impose paint etiquette rules and supervise the girls while they hosed down the porch. Then, no harm done, we returned to the more important business of solving the world's problems over tea and cakes, this time from the glider on the not-quite-so-white front porch.

I have been forever grateful to Barbara for this lesson in parenting. I don't think I could have kept my perspective or held my temper like she did, had I been faced with the same circumstances at my house. When your volcano threatens to blow, run and get the camera! It gives you time to calm down, think, and collect priceless pictures worth a thousand memories for years to come.

Late Bloomers

When our son Geoff entered kindergarten he was placed in a multi-grade classroom, a so-called K-1, which meant he would have the same teacher for both kindergarten and first grade. Parents clamored for this program's teacher, a well-trained, energetic and experienced man, one of the few male elementary teachers in the district. Our son liked this teacher very much, and they got along fine.

At the first parent-teacher conference I learned that Geoff's academic progress was steady, but he seemed distractible and inattentive. The teacher noticed that he seemed lost after assignments were explained, so he had to ask classmates what he was supposed to do. The teacher told me he frequently used the phrase, "Earth to Geoff," to get his attention, but he still couldn't sustain it.

We tried a number of interventions, including smiley-face stickers as rewards for improved attentiveness. By the end of his kindergarten year, Geoff had maintained his academic progress, but his listening skills were still weak.

When first grade began, I arranged to observe the class to learn more about Geoff's adjustment there. I noticed that his teacher presented assignments in an interesting and entertaining manner, but the noise level gradually increased after instructions were given, because students worked in groups and moved freely around the classroom. I could see that my son found the activity and noise level both distracting and confusing. The teacher circulated, providing additional instruction to individual students or to small groups as questions came up about their work. Geoff invariably looked up, curious about what others were doing rather than focusing on his work.

I recognized that he was floundering, so I requested a diagnostic evaluation. His achievement test scores were above average and some mild verbal memory problems surfaced, but nothing was statistically deficient enough to warrant intervention. Nevertheless, the special education teacher offered to work with Geoff one hour a week to help him improve memory/listening skills and, in the process, build up his self-confidence (which was starting to waver). He loved working one-on-one with her and would have accepted the help an hour a day if she had suggested it.

Geoff finished out the year as he had started it — strong academically, but weak in attention and listening skills. Always a physically active and athletic boy, he was overjoyed that school was over, so he could play sports all summer. As fall approached, he dreaded the start of second grade.

He was placed with another veteran teacher who had a reputation for identifying and building on individual student strengths. Every morning she put an agenda on the board and told the students exactly what they needed to do to complete each assignment. Next to the agenda, she listed learning activities that each child could pursue when finished with the assigned work and waiting for others to finish. Students worked independently, not in groups, and the teacher circulated to help each one.

This teacher soon discovered Geoff's strong visual/artistic skills and openly admired his detailed, realistic drawings of wildlife (he and a friend were ardent birdwatchers). She had a way of identifying special talents in each student and giving him or her recognition for them. By the end of the first month of second grade, Geoff's confidence was sky-high. He would have walked on water for that teacher, and so would I.

Both of these teachers were sensitive, positive and experienced educators. But one brought out our son's weaknesses, and the other brought out his strengths. Significant   differences between student and teacher learning styles or personalities may strongly affect learning outcomes for individual students. After all, learning problems don't always reside within the student. A spark, ignited between student and teacher, can often turn a pattern of underachievement around.

Parents usually know their children best. Therefore, when you have concerns about your child's academic progress or adjustment in school, contact his or her teachers to look for causes and develop solutions. Cooperation and persistence will most likely lead to effective changes.

Wild Tulips

Children learn early in life that language is power. A few well-chosen words can get a brother or sister in instant trouble. Ghastly tales about school or daycare trigger parental guilt just enough to get an extra dessert or a later bedtime. "No, Dad, I don't have homework tonight." How is Dad to know?

Parents don't know, of course, unless they take the time to call the school every day to check. Their only other choice is to teach their children about trust. Trust is a rather nebulous concept in the mind of a child. But each time words and behavior do not match, a perceptive parent can make the concept a bit clearer.

One afternoon Nikki, my first-grader, brought a toy food mixer home in her backpack. When I asked her where she got it, she told me that a friend at school had loaned it to her. I later found out she had taken it from school without asking. We spoke about words and trust after she spent five minutes in "time out."

Another time her daycare mother asked me whether I had been packing lunches for school each day because Nikki arrived in the afternoon asking for extra food, claiming that I had forgotten to pack her a lunch (which I had not).

"Hmmm. A clever ruse," I thought, "for sidestepping my rule about junk food and between-meal snacks."

That night we talked again after a longer "time out." She promised not to do it anymore.

A few days later, Nikki thoughtfully brought me a bouquet of tulips she said she had picked in the field across the street. Knowing that tulips don't grow wild and our garden had none, I asked her to show me exactly where she had found them. She led me into the field, pointed into the tall grass and insisted the tulips had come from "right there." Apparently serious talks and "time out" were but minor annoyances in the face of this power to create convenient realities with words.

"Perhaps if I can make the concept of trust less abstract," I thought, "my daughter will be able to understand its importance." I wanted her to know that earning someone's trust is just as satisfying, maybe even more satisfying, than manipulating people with words.

I took a long velvet ribbon and tied one end around my waist and the other around hers. "If I can't trust you when I can't see you," I said, "we'll just have to stay together."

It was a fun game at first, but when she got tired of helping me cook dinner, watch the news and make phone calls, she began to get upset. She wanted her freedom back and she wanted it now!

"I know what the ribbon means, Mom," she said quietly, as I gave her my end.

In those few minutes, the velvet ribbon had helped Nikki understand that honesty is something you carry with you always, even when other people are out of sight. Words can build trust or tear it down. To this day, some fifteen years later, my daughter's word is her bond.

Larkspurs

For his thirty-fifth birthday I bought Gordon a canary with a golden cage to match its feathers. We named him Fertz and wondered if he would sing. My husband discovered that if he whistled steadily while reading the paper, Fertz would sing along, a beautiful cascade of trills, chirps, and warbles. Wild birds sometimes perched on branches outside the window to harmonize with them.

In those days I taught private flute lessons. My students also wanted to entice Fertz to sing. We discovered that when they played their pieces through without stopping to correct wrong notes, Fertz would join in. I've never seen young musicians practice so hard!

Ah, motivation, that most essential yet unpredictable ingredient in the learning process. Teachers tell me that unmotivated students sadden and perplex them. They wonder what could have happened to "turn out the light" of curiosity and excitement about the unknown. Attitudes toward learning develop in the early years when children first encounter demands to master academic skills, especially reading — arguably the most important skill of all. Absent singing birds, how do teachers inspire children to persist during new learning?

I asked Jeanne, a friend who teaches first grade, if I could spend a day in her classroom — interacting with the children as well as watching her — to learn more about how she taps and maintains student motivation.

I arrived at about 9:15 a.m., one of four adult helpers that day. A child's parent was there to help out at the math center, and Jeanne's parents were also on hand to work with students at the computer and reading centers. I "floated" as an observer and helped students with whatever came up as they worked independently on different assignments. Jeanne taught several small group lessons.

Students worked alone, in pairs, or in small groups with quiet energy and purpose. The air fairly crackled with motivation, with nary a canary in sight! As students spoke with me about their work, I was struck by their efforts to seek creative math solutions and personal forms of written expression. Jeanne encourages divergent thinking, rather than a "right answer" approach.

Jeanne realizes how important parents can be as partners in her classroom — so much so that she invited her parents to work with her in class one morning a week.

Her father Andy has become the class computer consultant. He bought his first personal computer in 1985, shortly after retiring from the electric utilities industry. That was about six or seven computers ago, as expanded memory, power and speed made each successive model obsolete. Jeanne's first-graders eagerly caught the hand-me-downs. When invited to preview software, help set up the computers and teach the kids how to use them, Andy was happy to pitch in.

Claire, Jeanne's mother, has always loved listening to children. A college-educated woman and mother of three, she also wanted to express her interests and talents beyond the family. Helping first-graders strengthen their reading skills was one such opportunity.

Andy and Claire marvel at how quickly six-year-olds can master the complex functions of computer programs. They are thrilled, too, with the steady reading progress students make between visits. It's no mystery really.

For any child, an adult's delight is the canary's song.

C-c-crocuses

"I'm t-t-trying as hard as I c-c-c-can," Tanya stammered tearfully. "I just c-c-c-can't s-s-say it right."

Mrs. Bradford, the speech therapist, knew only too well how hard Tanya tried. Two years of twice-weekly sessions had resulted in no improvement. None of the techniques — relaxation, deep breathing, small group sessions, practice of individual sounds, singing — had diminished Tanya's stuttering. Her steadily increasing anxiety just made matters worse.

"Let's stop for today, Tanya."

Pure relief spread across the little girl's face. She managed a quick, "G-g-good-bye," before skipping back to class.

In search of another point of view about Tanya's lack of progress, Mrs. Bradford sought me out. I was one of the school psychologists with whom she had successfully collaborated in the past. We met over lunch and mapped out a new strategy that Tanya's parents readily agreed was worth a try.

Liza, one of Tanya's classmates, who was confined to a wheelchair, saw me weekly for counseling. Every other week Liza invited a friend to join her for a counseling activity, usually a therapeutic board game. The word was out that the games were fun, so Liza's friends all wanted turns to see the psychologist, too. Tanya was no exception.

When her turn came, Tanya wheeled Liza into my office, where Liza's assistant helped her onto the floor to play the "Talking, Feeling, Doing" game. Each player spins a numbered wheel, moves that number of spaces on the board, takes a card from one of three stacks, and responds to its message.

One of the cards Liza selected asked her to make a wish.

"I wish I could run and play like all the other kids can," she said wistfully.

A look of surprise and sympathy came over Tanya's face. "I wish you could, too, Liza," she said without a hitch. Tanya was so touched by the enormity of Liza's disability relative to her own that she completely forgot to worry about how she sounded. "I wish you could, too," she repeated.

After that day, Tanya's stuttering steadily diminished in direct proportion to her patience with herself. Liza's disarming wish caused Tanya to see her in a different light. She no longer perceived speech therapy as an embarrassment to be avoided. And Liza was the first friend she invited to join in.

Colt's Foot

Children must have invented Chinese water torture. If you have ever gone shopping for sneakers with a twelve year-old, you know what I mean.

The old pair has completely self-destructed, but he insists on wearing them to the mall anyway. He has to shuffle when he walks to keep them from falling off.

At Foot Fair we are confronted with a bewildering array of action footwear, each style custom-built for a different sport.

"Where are the Frisbee cleats?" I ask the salesman.

"Mooommm," Geoff groans. (He doesn't appreciate what he calls my "lame" attempts at humor.)

I turn over shoe after shoe, in search of a pair for less than $50. With a little luck I can find some name-brand closeouts on sale. My son, meanwhile, zeros in on the $80 specials with the "swoosh" on the sides.

Acting all grown up, he approaches the salesman to ask for a size 10. I, too, request two try-on pairs for him. Eagle-eye notices my choices, of course.

"Mooommm," again. "That one has black soles, which aren't allowed on our gym floor because they leave dark scuff marks. The other one isn't any good either. The soles aren't air cushioned."

"What does an air cushion do?" I ask.

"It provides more arch support and shock absorption than rubber alone and the 'swoosh' shoes have extra strength built into the sides."

"Geoff, half the time you don't even tie them," I say.

"That's only around home and at school, Mom. I tie them in gym," he counters.

"For two hours a week in gym, I think these other shoes will be fine," I assert logically.

"But, Mom. Look at the shape of the toes on them and the ugly zigzag stripes on the sides. I can't wear those. They look so ... so cheap!"

"Cheap? You call $50 cheap? I used to pay $10 for a pair of sneakers!" I can feel my face getting hot, so I take a deep breath and return to impeccable logic. "We have to buy new school clothes, too, you know. I can't spend everything on shoes."

I look up at the salesman, hoping for a nod, but he remains impassive.

"I don't want any new clothes," Geoff insists, digging in his heels. "I'll wear my old stuff."

"It's mostly torn or too small, Geoff."

"I don't care. All my friends wear old stuff. I can, too, so you'll be saving money."

I can feel myself weakening. School starts in two days; he has to have shoes; and I do want him to be happy.

"Oh, all right. Just don't start badgering me for those shirts you like with the special insignia on them that cost three times more than any other shirt on the rack. And   you have to clean your room when you get home."

Pathetic. I hate it when I give in.

"Wow! Thanks, Mom! Thanks a lot!" he says with that huge melt-my-heart smile. "They're awesome! Can I wear them home?"

I do like making him happy. Besides, if he doesn't mind look-ing a little scruffy on the first day back to school, it shouldn't bother me either.

On Monday morning we are all getting ready for school and work, when from the kitchen I hear, "Mom, come down here, quick!"

I find him walking back and forth across the linoleum floor in his new "swooshes." Squeak. Squeak. Squeak.

"Mom, listen to that. I can't wear these!"

"You can't wear them?" I ask weakly. "Why not?"

"They're so loud! Everybody will look at me! I'm wearing my old ones," he declares.

"But all new shoes squeak like that ... you have to break them in ... I paid $80 for those sneakers," I babble. "Just two days ago you had to have them." A loud groan issues unbidden from my throat as I head back upstairs to finish getting dressed.

Still within earshot, I hear Geoff ask his sister, "What's the matter with *her*?"

School Daisies

Got the schoolhouse blues? You are not alone. The last days of August top the charts for family peaks and valleys, as leisure time gives way to the anticipation of structure, expectations, peer pressure and competition at school. Many students, parents, teachers and principals get bogged down with self-doubts.

Students in special education ask themselves: "How do I explain the resource room to my friends? Does the fact that I have a learning disability mean I'm stupid? I sure feel like it sometimes. The extra help boosts my confidence, but then when I'm in regular classes, my confidence goes down. Other kids in my classes need help, too, but they don't have to go to the resource room to get it. Why me? It's so much easier to be on vacation. During the summer no one teases me. No one compares me to anyone else, and I fit in. But at school, I feel different. Why do I have to be singled out? Why can't the teachers just help me when I need it, without sending me out of the class?"

Parents fret: "I don't want to give my son medicine this year. He's been fine all summer without it. Maybe this year he'll be mature enough to handle all the assignments and commotion at school on his own. What if he starts to think that he can't succeed without medication? Will he think he needs alcohol or drugs to handle other challenges, too?"

"How I dread those complicated PPT (Planning and Placement Team) meetings with so many people sitting around a table talking about my child. Don't they know she's just like the rest of the kids? What do all those test scores mean? It's all so formal and legalistic. I feel like I'm in a courtroom instead of a school. Maybe I should just keep her home and teach her myself."

Teachers wonder: "How can I organize and present lessons so that every student succeeds? They're all so different, and their parents just don't have as much time available these days to help them. Maybe I should go back to graduate school in business or law, where I'd make more money and not lie awake at night. No, I'd miss the kids too much. I'll try harder to collaborate with parents this year."

Principals brood: "Every year the kids get rowdier and angrier. I never know when one of them will explode. Reports about school shootings are terrifying. I'd like to expel every student who makes a threatening gesture or remark, but I know that's not the answer. I have to set the right tone on the very first day: a tone of order, fairness, academic excellence, thoughtfulness, mutual respect and pride in our school. Whew! That's a tall order."

Students vow: "I'm going to study like mad this year. I fooled around last year and failed two subjects. I sure was embarrassed and so were my parents. They're right when they say that I'll never get into college if I don't take my studies seriously. It's up to me."

Got the schoolhouse blues? Make an appointment with a guidance counselor or school psychologist to talk about it. I have helped many students and parents work through school adjustment problems. Last fall I met regularly with a disgruntled high school student with a learning disability who needed to learn how to advocate more successfully for himself with his teachers. By the end of the year his failing grades had disappeared and in the final marking period, he made the honor roll. He started the next academic year with optimism and newfound confidence.

I have been fielding parent/student/teacher/administrator questions for years now and have helped them brainstorm solutions to many of the problems they face. We have learned a lot from each other ... including ways to chase the blues away.

Variegated Ivy

At the beginning of tenth grade our daughter Nikki met with her high school guidance counselor to discuss college preparation and entrance requirements. Since she had achieved nearly straight A's through ninth grade, she expected nothing less than glowing praise and encouragement to apply to Ivy League schools.

"Good grades are not enough, Nikki," the counselor told her. "If you want to compete for the top colleges, you need leadership experience, varsity athletics and more extracurricular activities. You need to build a résumé."

That was our introduction to the high school pressure cooker for college-bound students. Before that day, I held the old-fashioned notion that clubs and athletics were mostly for fun. A bit shaken but determined, our daughter followed the counselor's advice. She had always pursued personal interests in music, sports and community service, so she concentrated on finding leadership opportunities. Most of her friends did likewise.

The level of competition for admission to elite colleges and universities boggles the mind. Twelve thousand or more extremely capable students apply for every thousand admitted and they, too, have spent four years building their credentials. Dumb luck probably accounts for many of the "yes" decisions, because the quality of the applicant pool is so high. Toss out the top thousand and the second thousand look equally strong.

Ambitious high school students doggedly compete for recognition and class rank. With so much at stake, some kids buckle under the pressure and help each other cheat on tests, just to bolster their grade-point average.

One parent with whom I spoke about résumé-building was incensed. "My son's high school offers no course in trigonometry," she said, "but mandates thirty hours of community service before graduation." When she objected, she was told that colleges were more interested in seeing volunteer work than advanced math on his transcript.

Why are we subjecting our sixteen- and seventeen-year-olds to this kind of pressure when they are still trying to figure out who they are? Young people can feverishly beef up their academic and social service records, but emotional maturation takes time. Teens need long conversations, romance, hikes, journals, bike rides, poetry, fishing and daydreams, too.

Since people live longer, healthier lives these days, why not slow things down a little? Perhaps students should build their résumés *after* high school by taking a year or two away from their studies, to work, travel or help others. High school graduates could enter AmeriCorps, a domestic version of the Peace Corps, before college, to help revitalize inner cities and impoverished rural areas while gaining valuable life experience. Work apprenticeships also make sense, not only to save money for higher education costs, but also to help formulate career and study plans.

We need not push our children so hard that they become candidates for burnout before they even graduate from college. In the long run, the best-prepared college freshmen will be the ones who take the time to build some wisdom, wit and emotional maturity into their résumés.

Climbing Wisteria

A computer screen lit Terry's cubicle. Her eyes, too long unblinking, closed in relief as she pressed "Quit" and pushed back from the keyboard, finished at last. The transportation proposal, a masterpiece, rolled silently off the printer.

"Tomorrow's presentation in Omaha will clinch the account, as well as my future," she thought. "I doubt that our competitors can top this. In fact, I haven't met anyone who can develop better shipping plans than I can."

Sharing recognition with her co-manager for business deals that she closed without his help was getting old. Terry wanted a department of her own and the title to go with it. The word on the street, she knew, warned of a glass ceiling over women, an invisible barrier to top management positions.

"But times are changing. There has to be room in the corporate world for a top producer, woman or not," she told herself.

The following Monday, Terry made an appointment to discuss her ambitions with her boss.

"The Omaha manufacturer signed on with us this morning, Terry," Sam said. "Congratulations. Your proposals have brought in several large accounts lately. We need someone with abilities like yours to take over the logistics department of our West Coast Division. If you're interested, I'll give Ralph Glazer a call. He's my counterpart out there."

Terry left Sam's office on a cloud. She could hardly believe her good fortune. "Luck nothing, you've earned it, woman," she said out loud, smiling broadly.

The twenty-minute drive home seemed endless. She spent most of it rehearsing how to tell Walt the exciting news.

"San Francisco?" her husband exploded. "No way in hell can we afford to live there. No way."

"Listen, honey," she said. "I'll talk with Ralph Glazer about your concerns and he'll help us get the facts and figures about the cost of living differences between Detroit and San Francisco."

Ralph invited both of them to California for Terry's interview, all expenses paid. While Walt researched housing and sales positions for himself, Terry met with Ralph, who turned out to be a gracious host.

"Your track record is impressive; sounds like just what we need," he said. "Let me show you around, Terry. I'll introduce you to a few people."

As they walked through the outer offices, Ralph gave one of the secretaries a quick hug. "Hey, good lookin', this is Terry, a visitor from our Detroit offices." And so it went, from department to department, Ralph mixing teasing banter with information about the company. They ended the interview with a discussion of contract and salary, to be negotiated after Terry and Walt had a chance to calculate their financial needs.

After analyzing everything, they decided they would need about $35,000 more per year to make the move possible. It was more money than Ralph had offered, but Terry was sure he knew about the high price of housing, insurance, and taxes in the Bay Area.

She reached him from her office the following morning. "Walt and I have studied the figures, Ralph, and we've concluded that our monetary needs are somewhat higher than the guidelines you gave me."

"Doggone. Thanks for your interest, kiddo. Good-bye." Click.

Terry was sure she heard glass crack, as she sat in stunned silence with the dead receiver in her hand. Debriefing with Sam was nearly intolerable.

"No counter offer? Just doggone, kiddo, and good-bye? How unthinkably rude," he said. "He would never have treated a man that way."

They sat together, alone with their thoughts. As Terry rose to leave, their eyes met and held. From his sympathetic expression, she knew instinctively that Sam would be on the lookout for other opportunities for her. Her feelings of disappointment and fury began to dissipate.

Terry took a deep breath to steady her voice and said with conviction, "Wait until you see the plan I've put together for the Kansas City presentation, Sam. It'll knock your socks off."

After Terry told her dad and me about the abrupt breakdown in negotiations, we were disgusted with the recruiter's behavior, too, but not surprised. Even though women occupy more management positions in corporate America than ever before, gender bias still works against them to derail promotions and suppress earnings.

"He did you a favor, Terry," I said. "You wouldn't want to work for someone so backward anyway."

"That's for sure. It was their loss," Gordon commented. "How do you plan to handle this, honey?"

"Right now I'm really upset, Dad," she replied. "But I'm confident that my record speaks for itself. You, Mom and Beth have taught me to stand up for myself and maintain high standards, so that's what I plan to do. Thanks for the support, guys. I love you. Talk with you later."

Chapter Four
Pests

In gardening as in life, our best-laid plans often go awry.

Raccoons, I have learned, know exactly when corn ripens. The moment it is ready for picking, no fence is high enough to prevent these persistent animals from climbing over it and gorging themselves on ear after ear, until they are so stuffed their tail rings pop off.

My husband and I have tried every known remedy to protect our gardens from pests, but we no sooner get rid of one than a new one appears. Come to think of it, growing up is a lot like that. The obvious, superficial pests are easy to dispel; others dig in deeply and attack at the roots, taking single-minded determination to expose and eliminate before we can repair the damage.

Beetle Balm

Rotkäppchen, my little red Volkswagen, positively purred. She was the sassiest "bug" on the Autobahn, where she cruised along at 90 mph (downhill with a tailwind). Keeping her fed for European sightseeing jaunts, however, took more than ten-Pfennig bottle returns. I needed a job.

My German was passable enough to find work as a nanny with a Munich family, Herr and Frau Drexel and their twenty-month-old daughter, Monika. They paid me a decent wage plus room and board, and Herr Drexel also gave me German lessons. Each evening we listened to a half-hour radio program, which we discussed afterward. He sometimes told me stories about his life in the German army. I felt a bit unsettled to learn that he had been an SS officer during World War II.

Frau Drexel, a quiet and efficient woman, spent afternoons fixing delicious dinners and scrubbing the apartment, while Monika and I went sledding at a city park. Those were my favorite times with her, as we bundled up against the crisp cold air and whooshed down the hills together on our sturdy wooden sled.

A couple of months into this arrangement, as I contentedly saved my Pfennigs for late spring travels with Rotkäppchen, my father visited Munich en route to Amsterdam, where he was to present a paper about his chemical research. The Drexels invited him to their home for a traditional Sunday dinner of sauerbraten and dumplings.

After the meal, Dad and Herr Drexel talked, while Frau Drexel and I cleared and washed the dishes. Upon returning to the dining room toward the end of their conversation, I heard Herr Drexel say, "Well, we decided to keep Beth on despite her problems, because we know her mother is very ill."

I had no idea what kind of "problems" he could possibly be talking about. In shock, I said, "Perhaps you should ask me if I'm interested in your pity, Herr Drexel. Dad, I'll get my things. Let's go." We left immediately for my father's hotel.

Dad told me that Herr Drexel had been reading my mail, screening my phone calls, and even looking through my laundry. Unable to find any "evidence" against me, he expressed suspicions about my behavior and motives with men, apparently imagining things about a German college student I dated a couple of times while living there. Dad likened Herr Drexel to Captain Queeg of the *Caine Mutiny,* rolling steel balls around in his hand as evil thoughts rolled around in his mind.

This man hated me without even knowing me. He hated me because I was nineteen, American, and owned a car (which he did not). In his warped mind, his hatred was justified because Americans had won the war and occupied his country. I represented horrible events to him, namely the German army's defeat and his subsequent loss of stature.

It thrilled him to employ a naïve, trusting American girl over whom he could exercise power; it thrilled him even more to try to discredit and shame me in front of my father.

Prejudice was just a word without a face until I felt its sickening sting. Herr Drexel's blind prejudice changed my perspective forever. He had never intended to educate me; nor had he any genuine curiosity about me. He was blind to the real me. In his household, under his guidance, the precious Monika probably became blind, too.

As Rotkäppchen and I traveled on, a bit wiser and more watchful, I promised myself that prejudice would never darken my vision or my heart. Herr Drexel had educated me after all.

Flame Bushes

Hsss ... crackle ... The sounds awakened me from a deep sleep. I forced my eyes open. "Are those flames?" I wondered. "No, I'm just dreaming." I rolled over and tried to go back to sleep. Crackle ... hsss ... But it smelled like smoke and my eyes were burning. Oh my God, fire!

"Mommy, Daddy, Mommy, Daddy, the house is on fire!" I screamed, running down the upstairs hall to their room.

My mother emerged, sleepy and rumpled, squinting into the hall light. "It's OK, honey," she soothed, hugging me. "You're having a nightmare. Go back to bed now."

I walked cautiously down the hall and peeked into my room. Flames were licking upward beside my bed, making black soot tongues on the wall. "My bed's on fire!" I screamed.

The next few minutes jumbled with images: Dad beat on the mattress with wet towels. My brothers discovered my eight-year-old sister, still asleep in our smoke-filled room. (She was born without a sense of smell and virtually no hearing in one ear.) Mom hunched over the hall phone to call the fire department, speaking calmly, as if this were not a dire emergency! A siren wailed in the distance as my dad and brothers carried the smoldering mattress down the stairs and out into the yard. The firemen found them there, spraying it with the garden hose. Everything moved like molasses. Fear clutched me again after it was all over. I threw up to the smell of smoke.

A helper turned hazardous that night. My sister and I used a nightlight when we were younger. I guess we had stopped using it and forgot it was there. It must have broken when we pushed the bed against the wall after making it. The wires inside the broken bulb sent sparks onto the mattress, which then caught fire.

Today I can smell the slightest trace of smoke anywhere. That extra-keen sense of smell saved my husband and me from an equally unexpected fire. An oven mitt, ignited when he removed a pan from the oven and hung up over the stove smoldering but undetected, began producing smoke after we went upstairs to bed. Miraculously, my super-sniffer found the mitt just as it burst into flames over the stove. A quick dousing in the sink averted disaster.

We run fire drills at our house and play detective games with the kids to find hazards or potential hazards. A fire extinguisher on each floor provides more protection. Even so, we have had our share of close calls. Children go through stages of fascination with fire. They sometimes hide matches or lighters to experiment with candles, firecrackers, or cigarettes. Schoolteachers routinely address issues of fire safety. Parents should, too.

Fire is a tool like any other, although potentially more dangerous than most. We can teach our children and grandchildren to tame it, respect it, fear it, and use it safely.

Bleeding Hearts

Merengue and salsa music mingled with the conversation and laughter of migrant worker families, who had gathered to celebrate a successful sugar beet harvest before heading North where the tomato crop waited, ripe and ready for picking.

Gringo teachers organized this celebration each summer to say good-bye to the Chicano children, who attended school while their parents and older siblings brought in the crops. The children and teachers (I among them) had spent many hours transforming ordinary classrooms into crepe paper-festooned dining and dance halls.

Brightly colored papier-mâché piñatas shaped like tropical fish and farm animals decorated the school's main entrance. Inside, where the band played, stood cloth-covered tables, heavy under the weight of casseroles, salads, desserts and drinks that the county school district had provided for the partygoers.

Children and adults, young and old, brown and white, swayed and twirled to the contagious beat. The dancers' faces glistened in the late afternoon August sun.

Shouts, accompanied by staccato popping sounds, drifted in from outside. "They're breaking the piñatas," I thought, as I moved with the music toward the front door.

Suddenly, brown muscular arms grabbed my shoulders and held me against the wall, away from the doorway. "Don't move," the man whispered urgently against my hair. "Stay back."

"Let me go," I demanded angrily, trying to push him away.

He held me even tighter as screaming and more popping sounds erupted. Several people ran by us. Some dropped flat on the floor; others shouted orders.

"Abajo, abajo!" "Get away from the windows!" *"Tienen*

pistolas!"

The music came to a ragged stop.

Straining against the man's arms to look past him out the doorway, I saw a blue pickup truck speed away from the school. Two bare-chested men stood in the back gripping the side panels as the truck careened left onto the dirt road and disappeared in a cloud of gravel and dust.

In the quiet that followed, the man released me. I rushed outside along with several others to find out what had happened. Two young men lay inert in the schoolyard, one in the arms of a young girl, the other under the keening torso of his mother. An ambulance wailed in the distance.

Behind the violence was a lovers' feud. One of the men in the back of the truck had come to the party with armed friends to reclaim his girlfriend. They gunned down her new boyfriend and a cousin who tried to shield him. As they drove off they sprayed the crowd with bullets to keep people back. Miraculously, no one else was killed; two others were wounded.

Everyone but the girlfriend and mother remained eerily calm. We answered police questions; then we mutely worked together to put things away and clean up. No one wanted to leave. Shared disbelief and horror held us there, as did the comfort we found from each other.

I didn't start shaking until much later that night. Alone at home, my mind reeled with the sounds of laughter, music and screaming, the images of piñatas and the face of the stranger who had instinctively protected me from the bullets, the splashed blood and the motionless bodies. In that moment between life and death, cultural differences no longer separated us; protection of life itself was all that mattered. Had he reacted differently, one of those motionless bodies could have been mine.

Stinging Nettles

Taking care of children is far from easy. On the nights when a child fusses and cries, keeping everyone awake, a parent can feel ready to explode from exhaustion and irritation. Some parents take their frustrations out on their children. The excuses sound like this:

"I couldn't stand to hear her whine for one more second."

"He broke my glasses; I had to teach him a lesson."

"He knows I get mad when he begs for things, but he keeps right on begging."

"Swatting them is the quickest way to end their screaming tantrums."

But is a parent's disciplinary choice the child's fault? A ten-hour bumpy plane ride can produce identical feelings of anger and frustration. Yet some people who manage to grin and bear the plane ride, return home and whack their kids for spilling milk at the dinner table.

Thinking back to the years before I had children, I can remember two times I ever hit anyone in anger: once when my boyfriend refused to stop tickling me, and once when a girl in the neighborhood embarrassed my mother in public. In the first instance, I punched the boy as hard as I could on the arm. He definitely got the message and stopped pestering me. In the second, I chased after the girl and hit her with a belt across the legs. She ran home crying.

I am ashamed to say that my record as a parent is not quite so clean. I chose spanking as an option sometimes, to teach safety or respect for my authority. One evening, my two children were busy pushing all my "buttons" until I started the count to three. "One ... two ... two and a half...two and three quarters ... (they had never let me get to three before) ... three!"

I stormed up the stairs and confronted them in the hallway. Just as I brought my hand down to spank my son, he turned sideways. My hand met his hard hipbone instead of his soft derriere. Ouch, that stung! He ran into his room. Still furious, I spanked my daughter — too hard! Wailing, she ran off, too. I felt terrible about the whole incident. I went back downstairs to cool off and think.

About fifteen minutes later, I went back upstairs to apologize.

"I was wrong to hit you," I told them. "I will never do it again."

And I never did. From then on, I taught them that hitting others is wrong. I also showed them, by example, that there is always another way to settle a dispute short of resorting to physical aggression. Thankful that I learned this lesson, I hope my children have learned from my mistakes and will never physically lash out at anyone in anger.

But spanking is a time-honored form of discipline that teaches children to obey rules and respect authority, right? No. Spanking teaches children about aggression, fear and abuses of power; it teaches them nothing about respect. After I decided that spanking was no longer an option for me, I did not lose authority or respect. In fact, quite the opposite happened. I gained more of both, not only in my children's eyes but also in my own.

Shooflies

We were new in town, the only town of any size for miles around. "Centrally isolated," locals called the place, its main claim to fame an Ivy League college within its borders. With two master's degrees and extensive work experience, I was sure I could find challenging work in Ithaca, New York. "Not so," locals also told me. "Some of the clerks at JC Penney's and soda jerks at Ben and Jerry's have master's degrees, because there are so many graduate students competing for the few professional jobs around here."

I did not believe them. As a permanent resident whose husband had taken a position unaffiliated with Cornell University or Ithaca College, I presumed that I would have a distinct competitive edge over transient graduate students looking for work. As I had predicted, I landed several job interviews, all in my field, each requiring a person with my credentials.

One of the organizations sought a "Developmental Specialist" to evaluate the learning needs of young children (birth to five) with special needs. Having spent several years treating adults and adolescents in the private practice of psychotherapy, I was intrigued by the prospect of working with such young children and their families. I had closely followed the development of my own children, enthralled by the process of language acquisition and new learning of all kinds. In graduate school I had learned how to administer standardized IQ tests to preschoolers, but I had no idea how to assess the mental development of an infant. Imagine trying to measure the intelligence of a six-month-old!

My initial interview was with the director, who told me about the center and its programs, reviewed the sample test reports I had brought with me and introduced me to several members of the staff. All were friendly, knowledgeable and obviously committed to the center's intensive early intervention programs, which were designed to prepare special needs children for their fullest possible participation in society. All joined in to take me on a tour of their facility, an elementary school they had just purchased from the town.

Renovations were underway to convert some of the classrooms to offices and others to rehab spaces for occupational, physical and speech therapy services, leaving five rooms unchanged, to be used for toddler and preschool classrooms. The school was situated on a large tract of land with plenty of space to build a handicapped-accessible playground, already in the planning stages. Staff enthusiasm was infectious. I was pleased to find out that the center was strongly committed to ongoing staff training.

Toward the end of the interview, the director told me that finalists for the position would be asked to evaluate a child while parents and staff observed. After the evaluation I would be asked to discuss my impressions with the parent — also under staff observation. The test kit they provided was one I had never heard of, but I was assured that I could borrow it to prepare for the evaluation. I returned the following Friday to test a four-year-old boy.

On Friday morning I arrived early to review the child's records and set up my materials. I was assigned to a classroom that was lined with cardboard boxes full of materials, not yet unpacked because renovations hadn't been completed. Two cube chairs were placed in the middle of the room for the child — one to sit in and the other tipped on its side to serve as a desk. A low chair next to the cube chairs was in place for me — low so I could work at eye level with the child.

Danny, the four-year-old, entered the room running, his mother in hot pursuit. I helped her intercept him and guide him to the table in the center of the room. I hastily introduced myself and the observers to her before turning my attention to Danny, who had already popped up out of the chair and run over to the cardboard boxes along the wall.

"What's in these?" he demanded.

"Materials for the classroom," I said. "We won't be using them today. I have some neat things to show you in the little red suitcase over there. Come sit down and we'll take a look."

He obliged. I began a block stacking and imitation task with him with one-inch wooden cubes. He built an eight-cube tower with ease, then watched me build a three-block bridge and easily imitated that one, too. Next I built a five-block gate and asked him to make one like mine, but he lost interest and dashed to the cardboard boxes again.

He reached into one that was partially open and brought out a toy train on a string. He began to pull it along the floor, making chug-a-chug noises as he ran. All of a sudden he pulled up on the string and began to whirl the train around his head like a lasso, but he misjudged its path and it hit him solidly on the head with a loud whack. Everyone in the room winced except Danny. He just dropped the train, laughed and ran over to a full-length mirror on the wall, where I met up with him to check his head. There was a slight bump there, but he showed no sign of pain when I touched it. He shrugged me off and began making silly faces at himself in the mirror — then promptly spit on his image before scooting away.

I lured him back to the cube chairs with promises to draw some silly faces together on paper. We took turns drawing happy faces, sad faces, bodies and body parts. This activity enabled me to find out how well he could draw various shapes and how well he could represent human figures in his drawings. I tried out a few questions from the test manual while he was sitting at the table, but he refused to answer them. Within a few minutes he was off again, determined to delve into the contents of more boxes. I followed.

After rummaging through more boxes, mostly filled with children's books that he tossed aside, he trotted over to the windows to look outside. He stopped short of the windows when he noticed something on the black windowsill. Looking more closely, I realized that it was nearly covered with dozens of dead flies.

"What are those?" He asked.

"Flies," I answered.

"Cool," he said. "Can I touch them?"

"Wait, let's bring some over to the table," I suggested.

"OK."

I gave Danny a piece of paper to hold under the sill while I brushed the fly carcasses onto it with a second piece. With steady hands he carried them slowly to the table and gently set them down. We counted the flies, drew them, identified and counted their body parts, and talked about them for several minutes. Danny appeared relaxed and calm and was able to maintain his concentration throughout this activity; he even answered a few questions about opposites from the test manual before he folded his arms across his chest, shut his mouth tightly and shook his head, "No." He had had enough.

We did not complete many of the standardized test items, but I was able to learn a great deal about Danny's skills and learning style during this evaluation. His mother expressed relief that I had seen what she sees — that her son is extremely active and unpredictable. I observed many appropriate skills for a four-year-old, but I knew that he would have a hard time demonstrating them in a typical preschool classroom with twelve to fifteen children.

I learned a great deal about the center, too. The director and other staff members were more interested in how I handled the unexpected than in numerical test results (although some numbers would have been nice). They wanted to see how I answered the mother's questions, and how I interacted with her child.

When I left that day, I wasn't sure whether I had succeeded or failed in the staff's eyes. One thing was certain, however: this was an interview unlike any I had ever experienced, and one I never could have handled without the lessons in resourcefulness that motherhood had taught me. Apparently I succeeded more than I failed, because the next day the director offered me the job. I accepted. I later found out that the other finalist had tested a different four-year-old boy, who also wouldn't stay seated to take the test. After a few vain efforts to engage him with the test materials, the examiner closed his manual and test kit and pronounced the child untestable.

From seven years of evaluating children as young as five months old, I learned that building rapport, knowing how children develop and adjusting quickly to the unexpected are the most important skills for an evaluator of young children. We look for children's strengths and weaknesses and explain them as clearly as we can to families and others who work with children. The resulting profiles are far more useful for devising intervention plans than standardized test scores alone.

Some years later, during a conference presentation for school psychologists, I spoke about Danny and the process of evaluating young children. I reminded the audience that one's knowledge of child development is more important than any materials in the test kit. A gentleman raised his hand to comment.

"That may be true, Beth," he said, "but I think I'll add a small box of dead flies to my test kit — just in case!"

Perennial Flax

Life with an outspoken public figure is not for the faint of heart. My children and I can attest to that.

When Gordon and I married, he was the high school principal in Darien, Connecticut. I taught part-time at a Darien elementary school and gave private flute lessons on weekends in the district's music program. Other than the occasional question from a colleague about the scuttlebutt at the high school, no one leaned on me very often for privileged information. But when Gordon became the superintendent of schools in Wellesley, Massachusetts, I began to feel the heat.

Everywhere I went — restaurants, supermarkets, in line at the bank, at cocktail parties or the train station — townspeople buttonholed me. They sought my opinions about local issues in education and advice about how to handle problems with their children. I was flattered at first, until I realized they really wanted Gordon's ear.

"I'd be happy to give you my opinion," I learned to say. "If you would like to speak with Gordon about that, you can reach him during the school day at …" I then gave the person his office phone number.

When Gordon and I were out in public together, whether at public functions or running errands, people recognized him and continuously drew him into personal and political conversations (what Gordon refers to as "shoptalk"). We fully accepted this, at first, as part of his job. But it began to wear on us, to the point that we began doing business out of town and socializing with neighbors and friends who promised not to talk shop. It felt as if the larger community owned us around the clock.

Our children were one and four years old when we moved to Wellesley, so they were spared these "fishbowl effects" until they entered school. On the first day of kindergarten Geoff's teacher knelt down next to him and said, "I know you. Your daddy is my boss!"

For the next twelve years our children learned to anticipate a flurry of phone calls from both friends and complete strangers whenever snow began falling.

"Hi, Nikki" or "Hi, Geoff," they began. "Will you ask your dad if he is going to call off school?" One year Nikki got fed up with their badgering, so she started a false rumor to get back at them. Snow had begun falling in the morning and was intensifying by mid-morning. Nikki told each of the classmates who rushed up to her that she had just talked to her dad and he had promised to send everyone home at noon. Word spread fast, so when noon came, all the kids were eagerly awaiting the announcement that never came. Guess who got the last laugh (and less harassment) after that?

When Geoff reached middle school, a teachers' union contract dispute was raging. Some of the kids taunted him, saying that his dad was mean for not paying the teachers enough money. A few remarked that Geoff's good grades were "gifts" from the teachers, just to get on his dad's good side. Our son worked hard to achieve high marks in school, so the day a hockey teammate made a similar remark, Geoff said he felt as if he had been stabbed.

Gordon and I talked openly with our kids about school-related conflicts, trying to help them anticipate remarks from classmates and suggesting ways to handle them. They lost their cool once in awhile, but mostly we all grew more comfortable with the inevitable consequences of life in the public eye.

One time when Nikki was in middle school, a girl approached her in the bathroom and said, "Isn't it hard to be the daughter of the superintendent? Don't you wish you weren't?"

Nikki replied, "I'm very proud my dad is the superintendent. Wouldn't you be proud if he were your dad?"

We all laughed with relief and joy at that one. We sure were proud of Nikki!

The third time Gordon's contract came up for renewal in Ithaca, after six years in the district, a Board of Education majority voted it down. Headlines in the morning newspaper read, "Bruno Gets the Ax." Where was the executive editor's sensitivity? Geoff and Nikki had to go to school that day!

The following spring Gordon became a finalist for three different superintendencies in the Midwest, so we planned a whirlwind trip to visit all three towns in five days. While Gordon met with various community and school groups, I checked out school programs for Geoff and Nikki and toured each town with a local realtor. I also tried to get a feel for the quality of life in each community. Although not a requirement, Board of Education members like to meet the spouses of school superintendent candidates, so I was invited to a small reception and dinner with the board at the end of each day. Little did I know what kind of contribution I would make to Gordon's candidacy in the city of Rockford, the second-largest school district in Illinois.

On my way to meet Gordon at the central administration office after a day of information-gathering, I drove our rental car through a section of town where the traffic lights were on poles at the corners of the intersections rather than suspended overhead. Just as I got to the middle of one of these intersections (where I did not see the traffic light), I noticed a flash of yellow approaching rapidly from the left. I turned and saw a school bus bearing down on me. I accelerated, hoping to make it through quickly enough, while the bus driver slammed on her brakes to stop. Too late. The front bumper of the bus collided with the rear bumper and fender of my car.

Fortunately, neither I nor the driver or bus passengers were hurt. I was ticketed and fined $50 for "failure to yield." Shaken and embarrassed, but still able to drive the badly dented car, I joined my husband at the reception, where dozens of community officials were waiting to meet the candidate's "better half."

After I told Gordon about the accident, we immediately informed the Board, because we knew that a report might appear on the newspaper's police blotter the next morning or maybe even on TV later that night. Board members could not have been nicer. They told a few accident stories, too, and we laughed about the irony of the situation.

The next morning the story appeared in the paper all right, but not on the blotter. My run-in with that school bus made front-page headlines! Right beside the accident story was a small photograph of Gordon in his shorts, jogging merrily along the bike path that ran through the center of town, while members of the media interviewed him about his educational philosophy. I was mortified. Never have I wished so hard for anonymity, and we still had two more towns to go!

"Honey, aren't you glad you brought me along to help you make a good impression?" I asked Gordon as we headed out of town. "If I play my cards right, maybe I can get myself thrown in jail in Wisconsin."

Swamp Grass

We strapped a double mattress to the roof of the car, so that we could sleep in our new house the night before the moving van arrived with the rest of our belongings. But I couldn't fall asleep. Salty mucus kept collecting in the back of my throat, gagging me just as I was about to drift off. I tried a half-sitting position, but the tickle in my throat persisted.

The next day we thoroughly aired the place out, vacuumed everything and washed down the walls. With all of our furniture in place, we settled in for the second night. No luck. The mucus built up again and I lost another night's sleep. Benadryl was no help. My symptoms escalated to nausea and vomiting, which sent me scurrying to specialists for answers.

After I completed a multi-paged medical and environmental history questionnaire, the allergist confirmed my suspicions. "It doesn't take a rocket scientist to conclude that you're allergic to something in that house," he said. I had no history of allergies to anything. We discussed various possibilities. The most likely culprit was the aging high-pile carpeting throughout the house, "probably full of dust mites," the doctor hypothesized. He recommended that we remove it.

Reluctant to pull up five rooms of wall-to-wall carpeting, we started with the master bedroom. Sleep at last! But I couldn't tolerate sitting in other parts of the house longer than half an hour. When I began to suffer from repeated eyelid sties and eye infections, we took out the rest of the carpeting, thankful for the gorgeous oak floors underneath it.

My health settled down for several months, so we decided to re-carpet the stairs, thinking, erroneously, that dust mites had caused my allergic reaction. The symptoms returned. Everyone in the family it seemed,was suffering from more upper respiratory infections than usual.

Oddly, I could sleep comfortably in carpeted hotel rooms, friend's houses and various other places. So we began to look for other sources of toxicity in and around the house, thinking that my body might be reacting to multiple sources of irritation. We researched the subject and, one by one, began eliminating potential toxins.

We canceled pesticide and chemical lawn treatments, filtered the water supply to reduce chlorine content, installed special filters and a non-reservoir humidifier on the furnace (to eliminate the need for mold-retardant chemicals in the humidifier) and hired professionals to clean out the heating ducts. Step by step and year after year, in response to these and other changes, my health has improved. I've been infection-free for nearly two years now — the longest stretch without antibiotics that I can remember.

My theory is that everyone has sensitivities to environmental toxins, but we rarely inhabit places where the toxicity level is high enough to produce symptoms. When I entered an environment containing too many irritants for me, my system went haywire. Now that I know the signals, I can take corrective action quickly, no matter where I am.

When I look back at nights spent in hotels or in a tent in the backyard, I wonder how we ever got through it. It's torture to get sick over and over and have no idea what's causing it. The sleep deprivation was the worst part; I was a walking zombie for months.

I now pay extra attention to reports about environmental contaminants, because I have experienced their effects myself. Air- and water-borne irritants, chemicals in carpets and fiberboard, molds, dust, mites and mildew, aerosol and exhaust fumes are just a few of the hazards produced in industrialized societies. We need to reduce hazards in our homes, hospitals, schools and work sites in order to improve everyone's general health.

Shepherd's Purse

According to statistics from the Administrative Office of the U.S. Courts, the number of Americans filing personal bankruptcies surged past one million for the first time in 1996 and has remained over a million ever since. There were 1,242,700 bankruptcy filings in 1999. Most were personal property liquidations or Chapter 13 filings, which provide a shield while debtors and creditors work out repayment plans from available income.

These figures are especially puzzling in today's low-inflation, low-unemployment economy, which has produced increased amounts of disposable income. Furthermore, one of the consumer's biggest-ticket items, the cost of financing a home, has actually declined in many parts of the country, due to reductions in mortgage interest rates. Why, then, are so many households going belly up?

Because credit is easier to get than a sunburn. You don't even have to go out the front door for it.

Banks, department stores, and other companies repeatedly offer free credit by mail, phone or online to everyone on their mailing lists. Despite warnings from us, each of our teenage children fell prey to special credit card offers, which required no credit check, no current earnings and no adult signature. They intended to use their plastic sparingly, for the convenience of paying for midnight pizza delivery to their dorms, concert tickets or mail-order clothing. Charges expanded, however, to include long-distance telephone calls and airline tickets.

When our daughter got her first credit card bill for more than $300 she nearly fainted! She wisely cut her card into tiny pieces and got a part-time job. Our son charged past the credit limit on one card and promptly accepted another one, before he wised up and grabbed the scissors. It took him several months to get out of debt.

Bankruptcy no longer carries the social stigma it once did. You can even file the papers over the Internet! But make no mistake about it. Once in bankruptcy it takes ten years or more to reestablish credit. Some people are never able to clear their records.

It should be illegal to grant credit to poor credit risks, such as dependent students whose parents are footing the bills, the unemployed, and those who are already deeply in debt. Furthermore, the law should require companies that continue to issue credit to high-risk customers to cover the debt themselves when bills are not paid. Such a financial penalty would stop this practice immediately.

Society as a whole bears some responsibility to educate and socialize its young. Children are impulsive by nature; they want what they want when they want it. It takes maturity gained from experience to learn how to earn, save and budget money.

To the greedy credit card companies, I say, "Stop selling irresponsibility to our kids! Stop encouraging people to buy on impulse and pay for it for the rest of their lives!"

It is far easier to treat a sunburn.

Lamb's Ears

As a parent, I object to the gratuitous violence and explicit sexuality depicted on television and in the movies. Vivid portrayals of violence scare children and give them nightmares. Furthermore, impressionable children and teens have been known to imitate such behavior, because they lack good judgment and fail to understand the possible or probable consequences of their actions. TV and movie stars get away with it, they think; why shouldn't we? There have, in fact, been copycat crimes linked directly to specific TV programs and movies — a sobering thought for the actors, crews and studios that produce these shows and for the parents who allow their children to watch them.

American children also watch television to excess. The most insidious and pervasive consequence of the TV habit is the development of profound passivity in adults and children alike. A person watching a screen is usually physically inactive and psychologically unavailable for conversation, play, work, love, or any other form of interaction. We allow snippets of conversation during commercials, but how meaningful can they be, if we cut them off in mid-sentence four minutes later when the show comes back on?

People "zone out" in front of TV and movie screens, often ascribing more importance to people on the screen than to flesh-and-blood kids, spouses, pets, and pals. We are all guilty of it occasionally. My husband and I sometimes postpone working out our differences by turning on the tube to turn off the friction, at least for the moment.

Unfortunately, the screen habit begins so young that many children might never learn the fine arts of dialogue, fair fighting, creative story-telling, imaginative flights of fantasy, or the invention of activities with friends to fill precious hours of free time. Think of the satisfaction and pleasure derived from childhood hobbies, such as collecting stamps or baseball cards and trading them with friends. Do you remember the backyard carnivals and haunted houses, the sandlot softball and kickball games, and hot days at the local swimming hole?

When we got our first television (I was about six or seven at the time), we all welcomed it as a fascinating new form of entertainment, but it was by no means central to our social lives. In fact, it was often entirely too boring!

What do you suppose your family life would be like without so much video entertainment? Try a one-week blackout to see what happens, just to stir up some creative energy and animated, uninterrupted conversation. We tried it at our house and it was quite an eye-opener. We definitely became more interactive and interdependent. We invited friends over for dinner and games, did more reading than we had done in weeks, and discovered places in the state that we never knew existed.

Geoff and a friend of his redesigned the playing field for croquet. They built a tunnel over the rock garden with wickets at either end and placed one wicket next to the trunk of a tree that required a ricochet shot to get through. Every wicket received special treatment. The end result looked more like miniature golf than croquet. Turning off the TV sets certainly turned on their imaginations.

After spending many months of many years making inroads against TV zone-out in our family, video games, computers and the Internet made their appearance. What is a parent to do? At least the computer/Internet craze has turned out to be both interactive and career-enhancing. I never thought I would be drawn into it, but I cannot seem to get enough of cyberspace; it is such a fascinating and friendly place.

These days when my husband comes home from work, I hear, "Are you still sitting at the computer, Beth? That's where you were when I left this morning!"

"Yeah, Dad," the kids chime in. "Tell Mom it's our turn to get online."

We all laugh about Mom getting a dose of her own medicine, turn off the computer and head for the kitchen to make dinner together.

Chapter Five
Harvest

Parenting challenges never end, so take the time to congratulate yourself for making headway. Embarrassing moments will be counterbalanced by shining ones, like a child's well-deserved achievements in school, athletic victories, new best friends or the occasional, "Thanks, Mom... Thanks, Dad."

You've labored in the fields and produced a bumper crop. Let the soil rest while you celebrate the harvest. Planting tomorrow's seeds can wait.

Bean Sprouts

"Mom, can we have lunch in the garden?"

"Sure, boys. Just leave some ripe treats for Nikki. She's bringing a friend over for lunch, too."

Geoff and David scampered down the hill to the family garden, opened the chicken-wire gate and began snacking on plump strawberries, lettuce and sugar snap peas right off the vine. No mother could complain about the nutritional value of those munchies!

Planning our snacking garden was great fun. We found a level, sunny patch of ground next to some birch trees at the edge of our backyard, away from the swings and sandbox. After hauling some old railroad ties down there to establish the perimeter of our plot, we started to dig. Clank! And dig some more. Clank!

New England soil, we discovered, has more rock than dirt. Removing all the grass, weeds and rocks was the hardest part of the whole project. It took six of us — Gordon and I, Geoff, Nikki and two of their friends — two solid days of digging and raking to prepare the dirt for its special fertilizer — several wheelbarrow loads of aged horse manure from our neighbor's shed. We mixed it into the soil thoroughly.

At first the kids wanted to plant one of every edible plant they saw in the seed catalog, but our garden was too small, so they settled on foods they could eat raw. That eliminated a few, like asparagus and rhubarb. They loved carrots, so we included a row of those, even though that meant cleaning and peeling before eating. They added bush beans to their list, and strawberries, blueberries, lettuce, spinach, cucumbers, cherry tomatoes and sugar snap peas, the kind you can eat right off the vine, pod and all.

We showed the kids how to plant shallow rows of seeds and cover them with about an inch of soil. They poked a stick through the end of each seed packet and stuck it in the ground to identify each row's crop. We bought two flats of strawberry plants that had already rooted and arranged them over several raised dirt mounds in one corner of the garden. Two small blueberry bushes occupied another corner. I secretly buried a few "surprise" seeds, just for fun.

Finding volunteers to water the garden regularly was never a problem, because the child with the hose not only doused the fruit and vegetable plants, but also sprayed every other plant and person in sight, to a chorus of squeals and laughter.

We didn't have to wait long. The soil in that garden was so enriched by the horse manure, seedlings nearly burst from the ground overnight. The strawberry plants produced fruit first, because we had started them from established plants. The kids, their friends and every passing bird tasted those bright red, juicy berries. Unfortunately, little critters nibbled away the spinach leaves as soon as they broke ground, but everything else grew in lush and delicious. We snacked in the garden all summer long.

The "surprise" seeds grew large fan-shaped leaves that hid a bumper crop of squash, each one round and plump and nearly as long as my arm. Holy zucchini!

Sunflowers

A coffee mug, a piece of fancy paper, and a silky red tassel. That is what our son has to show for his $99,000 liberal arts education ... at least on the outside. On the inside, the changes are priceless.

He left home, all six-feet-four inches of him, worried that his roommate would have two heads of green hair and the professors would cover his carefully constructed papers with red ink. These are two of the fantasies he shared with us about what this highly regarded, demanding college would be like. The others he kept to himself, but you could see the wheels whirring behind his shy, watchful eyes.

Not that he had been sheltered. He did his share of traveling, attending summer camps, and taking bike/backpacking trips with friends and relatives. Somehow this was different. It was the beginning of preparing for adult life, and he had no idea what he wanted to choose for a profession. Also, he was still a boy inside that man-sized frame, with grand dreams for success and recognition, dreams much easier to believe were possible when in the company of best friends and family. Would he make his parents proud? Would he be accepted and respected by fellow students? Would he make the varsity hockey team? What about fraternities? What about love?

Now, four years later, he has graduated. He is still six-feet-four-inches and still looks about the same on the outside. But there the similarities end. His gaze is steady and calm. His academic record improved every semester even as he took increasingly challenging courses. One semester alone he was assigned 18,000 pages of reading! He quickly learned how to read for essentials. Through interaction with students and faculty from all over the world, he has shaped many fundamental, strong opinions and values. He can express himself eloquently and fervently, face-to-face or on paper. He is thoroughly conversant with cyberspace. And, yes, he even found love.

Our son has become a man. How can you put a price on that?

Yet price it we must, and $99,000 is too high. Over the past thirty years, college costs have spiraled out of control. When I attended the University of Michigan in 1963, tuition was $100 per semester. Even private universities charged about $1000 per semester then. Today, many of our students are graduating from college saddled with debt, their families' resources tapped to the max. The costs of continuing on to graduate school loom ever larger.

Our young people need education beyond high school to acquire the knowledge, skills and maturity to compete in the world today. We cannot afford to let our colleges and universities become provinces for the wealthy elite; we need to find ways to make them affordable for all. Then everyone who is willing to work for it can earn that mug, piece of paper, and tassel while making the stunning transformation from childhood to adulthood.

We now guarantee our children a free public education until age sixteen. What about extending the age to twenty-one? Let's make education beyond high school a right, not a privilege.

Pumpkin Seeds

The story of Cinderella has given stepparents a bad name. The ugly stepmother treats Cinderella like dirt and her two haughty daughters like entitled heiresses. The three of them are a greedy lot, contemptuous of dutiful, kind Cinderella. The ugly stepmother lusts after the king's riches, which she is sure she can get her hands on by finagling an engagement and marriage between one of her daughters and the king's son.

Where does this story leave stepparents in real life? That "ugly" modifier haunts them. There is bound to be something evil about a stepparent, the kids think. In truth, being a stepparent is to live in no man's land. You can't discipline the kids because, "You're not my dad! ... You're not my mom!" If you have kids of your own, then, "You love them more than you love me!" chant the stepchildren. If you truly love your second spouse, "You're trying to take my mom (or dad) away from us!" You can't win.

The divorce and remarriage rates have been so high in the last thirty years that most families probably have at least one or two stepparents. Most stepparents are eager to mend fences, love their blended family members, and hope for continued, genuine bonds between the stepchildren and their original parents. Blood bonds are sacrosanct. No adult wants to see children suffer rejection from their biological parents, and would only interfere if that parent were mistreating his or her child.

Personally, I am very thankful that my father finally remarried after living alone for nearly twenty years following my mother's death. I tried for years to match him up with divorced or widowed friends, to no avail. He is such a fine, vibrant person with so much to offer a companion and mate. I never could understand why women weren't chasing him. Maybe they were and he just wasn't ready to get caught!

Now he has a fantastic partner. They have been married for more that fifteen years and have put tremendous energy into loving each of their many children, grandchildren, and great-grand-children. It has not always been easy to blend our families at re-unions, but over the years we have grown steadily closer, less wary and protective, and more accepting and caring toward one another.

Try sharing your stepparenting experiences with others. I hope you will take the risk, because our children can learn to set aside their suspicions and fears of new adult "intruders" in their families if we, their parents and role models, can.

I know from personal experience as a stepparent that the "ugly stepparent" fairytale archetype is present, damaging and unfortunate. My stepchildren have been grappling with it for years. At long last, as adults themselves, they now love me for who I am, rather than as a caricature of fiction.

Morning Glories

Sunday is my favorite day of the week. It begins with classical music, breakfast, and the *New York Times*, an exquisite trio of sensations. The luxurious harmonies of a symphony mingle with the aromas of freshly ground coffee, crackling bacon with eggs, and toasted homemade bread. I linger over page after page of international news, fashion and travel until I reach the irresistible nugget toward the end of the magazine section: the crossword puzzle. The worse the weather, the cozier the Sunday; sounds of wind and rain rattle the shutters and wrap me in.

Classical music has stirred my soul since infancy — my son's, too, in utero. As I drove to orchestra rehearsal, he slept, only to awaken and celebrate as soon as the maestro's baton came down. It was a bit distracting to my fellow musicians to see my belly keeping time with the percussion section — he kicked especially vigorously during brass fanfares.

Throughout childhood, beginning in elementary school, I played the piano and flute. My friends and I marched in the band, played in the orchestra, and saw every live production of opera, jazz, ballet and symphony that came to town. We performed in school and community theater productions, too. It seemed like every kind of entertainment was popular enough to draw a crowd.

Today, tight school budgets, fewer classical radio stations, and rare TV broadcasting of classical performances have reduced exposure to the classical arts, both as participants and observers. Many schools offer only vocal music at the elementary level, which means students aren't being introduced to instrumental music until middle or high school. Through no fault of their own, the quality of music some of these late starters make is so abysmal, they're embarrassed to perform for friends and family. As a result, many of them simply stop playing.

A friend of mine, who conducts choral music, has noticed a decline in young listeners at classical concerts. They aren't interested in coming because they know so little about the music. She showed me an article from the magazine *Voice of Chorus America*, which described a clever way to pre-educate audiences about concert programs. Called "Dial a Preview," people use their telephones to hear a three-minute audio program about upcoming concerts. In a test run before a Minnesota choir's final concert of the season, more than a thousand people dialed the preview, resulting in a standing-room-only crowd for the first time ever. Concert promoters were correct in their thinking that people rarely buy tickets to something unfamiliar, but they will buy in great numbers when they know what to expect.

Live entertainment stirs the soul in ways no recorded or taped renditions can. It is a tremendous loss to our young people to miss experiencing the incomparable beauty of the classical performing arts. We must bring them to the well over and over again, where eventually they will drink long and deeply. Their favorite days will be enriched for it.

Shrinking Violets

To get a weekend pass off hospital grounds, you had to gain weight. Some patients taped quarters to their inner thighs to add a few extra ounces. Others drank several quarts of water just before weighing in. People with anorexia knew all the tricks of rapid weight control, like taking diuretics or laxatives to get rid of weight quickly or purging themselves of forbidden foods with self-induced vomiting.

My stepdaughter Cindy, who has suffered from an eating disorder for more than twenty years, traces it back to her mid-teen years, when there was a major upheaval in her family. Her mother, a divorcee for ten years, met and fell in love with Raymond, a wealthy surgeon, and decided to remarry. Three of the couple's four children were away at college, and Cindy was in high school.

Moving in with Raymond meant changing high schools, too. His huge house with sumptuous grounds and swimming pool, a bedroom decorated to her specifications and a private phone line did nothing to quiet her longing for old high school friends and the security of the small apartment community she had called home for ten years.

She was happy for her mother and Raymond, but the two of them were so wrapped up with each other that she felt alone and abandoned. They grew increasingly impatient with her moodiness and accused her of being selfish and inconsiderate. To appease them she covered up her misery as best she could.

One particular occasion stands out in Cindy's mind. During her parents' wedding reception, catered at her stepfather's house, she was taking something out of the refrigerator, when a guest approached her and introduced himself. At one point in the conversation he said, "You know something? I've never seen a girl eat so much in my entire life." That comment, Cindy later told me, made something click inside her. She felt ashamed by the perception that she had lost control in public in front of a complete stranger.

The next day she put herself on the Scarsdale Diet. She became obsessed with following it to perfection. She monitored her progress using litmus paper strips to test her urine — the darker the strip's color, the more weight she would lose (as she interpreted the diet book). This was her proof that the diet was working and proof that she was in control. She wrote out a list of foods that she allowed herself to eat and lost far more weight than was healthy for her. If she ate a "forbidden" food, she felt like a caged lion until she forced herself to throw it up.

Raymond and her mother grew increasingly concerned. They made delicious meals for her and hovered nearby until she finished them. They wouldn't let her use the car unless she gained weight, a tactic that made Cindy feel even more trapped. They took her to a therapist, but after several months of psychotherapy with no improvement, they admitted her to a hospital. Many years of treatment followed, as Cindy's family, friends and husband helped her wrestle with this persistent, dangerous disorder.

Cindy looks back now on all the years of obsession with eating and realizes that she became food phobic, that is, literally afraid of many foods. She is still thin, but eats a healthier diet and has stopped the bingeing, purging and starvation cycle. Her ongoing recovery process includes advice from a nutritionist and weekly meetings with a support group.

Society's emphasis on thinness played a role in Cindy's condition, because she equated weight gain with looking unattractive. She was also a gymnast and the coaches emphasized weight control. Cindy thinks that many girls get temporarily caught up in competitive weight loss for dance class or sports or to wear a size 5, but they get over it, accept their body type and move on. That didn't happen for her. She views her eating disorder as an addiction that became all consuming. It also masked feelings of sadness, loss, anger and low self-worth, which she has uncovered and explored in therapy. Ever vigilant, yet ever stronger, Cindy strives for personal growth in other parts of her life now, as a professional and as a parent.

Grape Vines

The neighborhood roots are moving next Friday. Their house has been sold. The kitchen table that has absorbed the tears, the fisted blows, and the heat of twenty-five years of soothing teas will soon squeeze into the back of an overloaded Ford station wagon bound for Michigan, a thousand miles away. With it will go a woman of unselfish generosity and wisdom, who has been the soul and glue on our block for all these years.

Other families have come and gone; she and her family stayed. Almost every day, it seems, one of us agonized over decisions and sought valued advice at that table. She helped us figure out how to cure allergies, learning disabilities, and shyness; how to inspire talent, resolve marital spats, and even tame unruly animals.

Then, quite unexpectedly, her husband lost his job as vice-president of an advertising firm. Hope kept them going for the ensuing four years of unsuccessful job hunting, while they steadily depleted their savings and their marriage. Neither survived. After four years of torment, our friends will start separate lives.

One more casualty of the recession, this family is scattering. Extended family will house the woman, her younger daughter, and their dog and cat. Her ex-husband will live with friends and work as a department store clerk while he continues to search for work more appropriate to his background. Their two older children, a son in college and a married daughter, live in other parts of the country. They have planned visits to their mother, father, sister, and extended family to give and receive needed love and reassurance. People cope somehow.

We were lucky to have such stability in our midst for so long. No one seems to live in one place for longer than ten years anymore. Rarely do we have the luxury of making lifelong friends, especially whole families of lifelong friends. Instead of putting down deep roots in one place, we are learning to spread horizontal ones across the miles, nourishing them by mail or phone.

That is what we can offer our friend now. Through our network of friends and family members we can help her find another neighborhood for her table. This is no time to feel sorry for ourselves for our loss. It is time to share with her what she shared with us: the capacity to be a true friend.

"A friend is one to whom one may pour out all the contents of one's heart, chaff and grain together, knowing that the gentlest of hands will take and sift it, keep what is worth keeping and with the breath of kindness blow the rest away." — Arabian proverb

Marigolds

Early in our marriage my husband and I never watched the Friday night fights; we produced them. After storing up all our grievances for the week, we would have dinner, begin talking and wind up screaming at each other. Our conversations weren't meant to deteriorate like that. We were trying to be honest with each other.

"I'll give him some constructive feedback."

"I'll help her understand me better."

"Open lines of communication are at the heart of a good marriage," we had read. We looked to our immediate families for role models.

My parents married at age twenty-five and had five children by thirty-one, without a single set of twins! At thirty-seven my mother contracted an incurable illness that gradually stole her vitality and steadily increased her dependency on Dad and us kids. We learned about compassion and love through adversity from them.

Gordon's parents divorced when he was two. He and his brother were raised by their grandmother, while his mother worked long hours to support them. His mother later remarried a kind, loving man who adopted the boys; but the marriage faltered, only surviving for the sake of the children. We learned about sacrifice and commitment to children from them.

Taking what lessons we could from family and friends, we knew we wanted to create something lasting, but we also knew that we would have to figure out how to do it in our own way.

Our weekend arguments cleared the air, but otherwise were just plain unpleasant. He felt like I was trying to change him, and I thought if he loved me, he would want to change to make me happier.

"I'm growing weary of this conversation," he would say, before lapsing into stony silence. Unable to pry another word out of him, I would stomp off to another room.

Thankfully, we usually recovered from nasty Fridays by Saturday morning, which saved the weekend for adventures together or with family and friends. Privately we thought about the previous night's grievances, swallowed our pride, and tried to change just a little. We hated those fights. And loving each other was much more fun — even more so when we decided to have babies.

To us, children are irresistible. Sharing in their lives has been the most absorbing, gratifying activity we have ever undertaken. But as much as we love the company of our kids, we sensed that we needed to find time alone together. So once a year we take a short vacation, just the two of us. No matter how complicated, expensive or inconvenient it is, we always manage to get away for five to seven days, usually in the winter to someplace warmer, to play.

To make these trips more affordable, we often register for a national education conference and add a few vacation days to the end of it. While Gordon attends workshops, I scope out the city for entertainment on the extra days. I usually listen to keynote speakers at the conference and meet Gordon's colleagues at evening receptions, events we both enjoy and can attend together. Combining professional development and a short vacation pays for one flight and a few nights at the hotel; and we cover the rest.

These, then, are our secrets after thirty years of marriage:

- Fight it out (words only, no fists).
- Give in a little (you don't have to admit it).
- Make peace.
- Refuse to quit.
- Have kids only if you want and love kids.
- Get away, just the two of you, once a year.
- Smooth over the rough spots with endless amounts of fun
     — together or with family and friends.

Beach Plums

Whole families need getaways, when they leave their busy schedules behind to relax, enjoy shared experiences and discover things about each other that they may not have known or noticed. My brother and his wife found an idyllic place along the shores of Lake Michigan — an A-frame cottage with no phone and no TV — where our growing clan has vacationed together every summer for almost thirty years.

People who have never seen the Great Lakes have no idea how vast they are. The restless waters stretch as far as the eye can see, like a freshwater ocean rimmed with shifting dunes and beaches of fine sand that zings underfoot. Although the waves usually lap gently against the shore, wild summer thunderstorms stir up huge breakers that can topple grown men and pull them under. The water temperature varies widely, too, depending on the prevailing winds. We plunge into 75-degree waters that flow up from the south or gasp and retreat from 55-degree waters blown down from the north — even in the middle of August.

Collectors all, we comb the beaches for indigenous treasures, such as Petoskey stones (fossilized coral), sand dollars and select pieces of driftwood to craft into lamps, tables, picture frames and other artifacts. One year my brothers found part of a tree trunk washed up on shore, ball of roots and all, which had been smoothed in the surf and bleached white by the sun. They attached ropes to it, dragged it halfway up the dune to the cottage and rested it lengthwise between the house and driveway. It became the base of a huge driftwood sculpture that received dozens of added "finds" over the years and now stands as a welcoming structure to all visitors. The curly, twisted roots, jagged trunk and odd collection of branches create a dramatic silhouette against the sky that is not only striking but also functional, doubling as a drying rack for wet bathing suits and towels.

Grandparents, parents, aunts, uncles, cousins, friends, children and grandchildren spend as much of the two weeks set aside for our family gatherings as they can. The accommodations are tight but manageable. Youngsters roll out their sleeping bags on the floor of the upstairs sleeping loft; two people get the living room futon; others pitch tents on the surrounding dunes. Still others book rooms in nearby motels and resorts.

No matter when we arrive, we quickly ease into the flow of activities. Marathon bridge games and jigsaw puzzles are underway in the common room amidst chatter about favorite books, music and songs. Every visitor signs up for one or two days of meal planning, preparation and clean-up (dinner only — we graze for other meals), an equitable way to divide the labor so that everyone does his or her share. Small groups take long walks along the beach or into the woods. Others join excursions for dune buggy and bumper-boat rides or set off on blueberry and cherry picking runs. The inveterate golfers head for the links.

After a big buffet dinner — usually a main dish plus fresh corn on the cob, salad, bread and homemade desserts — many of us trek up the steep dune behind the cottage. From the top we can look out over the landscape and across the shimmering lake to the horizon, where water and sky meet to snuff out the blazing sun, its after-glow bathing the sky in pink, orange, yellow and gold. Evenings are for bonfires, dancing, music, charades, skinny-dipping or whatever else we fancy. Before falling asleep, we watch for falling stars or meteor showers, quite common in late August.

Family getaways stimulate much more than fun and games. Beach walks and midnight talks often lead to discussions of problems, too. One year I had been troubled by nightmares. Talking with family members about it really helped, because a few of them had gone through similar bouts. Not only were their personal revelations reassuring to me, but the conversations also helped me pinpoint when the dreams started. From there I was able to bring some of my fears into the open and quiet them. Precious support, given and received, can make just about anyplace special to a family.

Over the years, my brother Dick and ex-wife Lucy's daughters have invited friends to join our gatherings. One of them was so moved by the setting and the pleasure of his experiences with us that he composed this poem in our honor:

Let us Bless the open spaces, huge and small
That hold us in their handfuls as the
Sun streams shadows across the ridges of the windfall light
And bark and green and sand and airy
Blueness twist into our Landscapes

Let us Bless the Play and power of the Waves,
The sum of one thousand and one watersfalling
As they tickle and tumble the toes and torsos of
Young and Old

And Let us Bless the Old as they taste Youth again with
Relish and not forgotten splendor
And the Young as they overcome picky-eating
Or merely meager rations to savor the wisdom
That sometimes flourishes with age, again, again,
Against the somber-hued A-frame backdrop
On meadowed inclines

And Let us Bless this fulsome, bawdy bunch of bustling
Bru'ha'ing Baumans as they bounce and snuggle their way
To laughter which rises like the Sun's steam
And clings to the walls and A-Frame to
Rest fondly on the eaves of memory

— Steve Gibb, August 1986
Gibb is the author of *Twentysomething, Floundering and Off the Yuppie Track,* 1992, Fawcett Press.

Snapdragon Puppets

I have often wondered why there are gaps in our memories; why some memories are so vivid and others so vague. I find it puzzling, for example, that I can recall the names and picture the faces of every one of my elementary school teachers except one, that of my first-grade teacher. Oddly, I have no recollection of first grade at all, even though memories of kindergarten, Bible preschool and other early places and events run through my mind in full color.

Out of curiosity I decided to find out what was going on in my family when I was six years old. My father told me that back then my mother had been experiencing unusual physical symptoms of fatigue and weakness in her legs. After several medical tests were completed, a tentative diagnosis was made: multiple sclerosis, a progressive, incurable disease of the central nervous system. As her symptoms persisted and the meaning of the diagnosis sank in, my mother grew increasingly frightened and despondent, while trying to hold onto the hope that the doctors could be wrong.

My parents decided to seek a second opinion about Mom's condition from specialists in Cleveland, where they grew up. During the weeks she was hospitalized there for diagnostic tests, Dad returned home to Michigan to take care of my three brothers, my sister and me. It was such a traumatic time for the five of us that not one of us remembers a thing about it. My oldest brother, who was eleven then, has a vague recollection of flying home from Cleveland at about that time but can't remember why he was there. We had all erased those weeks from our minds, even though Dad drove us all to Cleveland to bring Mom home!

"Don't you remember playing in the elevators at the clinic?" Dad asked me. "We were frantically searching for you everywhere!"

In contrast, my mother's siblings, who still lived in Cleveland then, vividly remember her arrival, hospitalization and their daily visits to her bedside as if these events had just happened yesterday.

Shortly after Dad and two of my mother's sisters told me about those eventful weeks, I began to experience wave after wave of buried memories, a kaleidoscope of early images of my mother ... brushing and braiding my hair ... teaching me how to pinch the blossom of a snapdragon to open and close its "mouth" like a puppet ... helping me learn to read my first sentence, "How big I am!" even before I went to school. Those memories, accompanied by the sound of her melodious laughter, are precious to me beyond words.

I have since met more of my mother's relatives, who had long been but names on the family tree. Now they are part of my life and the lives of my husband and children. My mother came from a family of eight children, who scattered across the country over the years to raise families of their own. After my mother's death from multiple sclerosis, which occurred when I was twenty years old, I had gradually lost touch with most of them. I had never met many of their children and grandchildren. Reconnecting with them now is changing all that.

Filling in my first-grade memory gaps has given me a sense of continuity with my past. It has also led me to wonderful, loving people who knew my mother when she was a child. They have taken me to the neighborhood where she grew up and shown me some of her poems and paintings that I never knew existed. And, best of all, they have welcomed my family and me warmly into theirs. All I did was wonder, out loud, about a year lost from my memory.

Chapter Six
Regeneration

After my youngest child left for college, I discovered pockets of curiosity and drive that took me in new directions I never would have contemplated twenty-five years ago. Had anyone told me I would become a professional writer, I would have shaken my head in disbelief. I scarcely had time to correspond with friends, let alone write for a living.

Now hundreds of ideas clamor for my attention. I had better buckle down and put them on paper before my next career change. You never know!

Creeping Buttercups

A nasty bug struck our family recently and sent us dragging to our doctors for treatment. Before I saw mine, the nurse asked me to get on the scales, which climbed higher than at the end of my last pregnancy, over twenty years ago. I nearly fainted.

Aside from the indisputable fact that doctors buy scales from a special factory that calibrates them to read ten pounds heavier than true weight — just to SCARE the pounds off you — I knew with even greater certainty that my well-honed rationalization skills had met their match ... FAT. It really does sneak up on you.

To make matters worse, blood test results from my annual physical a month later indicated that my cholesterol and triglycerides were on the rise, too. Help! I still wanted to believe the rules from the infamous chocolate chip cookie diet. First you eat the usual low-cal foods (grapefruit, spinach, Melba toast and fish) for breakfast and lunch. Then you can chow down on garlic bread, pizza and cookies for dinner, provided that you:

- Eat alone. If no one sees you eat it, it has no calories.
- Eat less at parties than the people around you and serve them fattening foods.
  When they gain weight you look thinner.
- Break food into tiny pieces. The smaller the pieces, the fewer the calories per piece. This is called cutting calories.

The teenage rebel in me (gone but not forgotten) loves this diet!

At the moment, however, this subject is no laughing matter. The mind games must stop. No more telling myself I can eat more because I walked eight laps around the track this morning. No more skipping dinner for dessert, just to reduce calories. Those perky, irritating health gurus are right; there really are no substitutes for less consumption and more exercise. From now on I need to read food labels for every detail about nutritional content and crank up my heart rate at least a half hour every day.

Years ago I could drop five pounds in a week if I worked at it. My husband says he lost as many as five pounds a day when playing college football and put them right back on later that night. But quick-fix approaches, like fad diets, are mind games, too. They just don't last.

Body weight might only be a number on a chart, but it represents so much more. It ties into feelings about aging, mortality and self-image. Perhaps recapturing my slimmer self will turn back the clock some. It certainly will be an important step toward conquering a quietly self-destructive habit. Fat, after all, harms the body as insidiously as smoke, drugs, or alcohol can.

That nasty bug hit me harder than I thought. And my doctor didn't even mention the scales. She let the FAcTS speak for themselves.

Lady Slippers

Sam hung around the Aragon ballroom in Chicago when he was seventeen, drawn by the big band sound, the glittering chandeliers, and the beautiful girls gliding across the immense ballroom floor. Light touches, one under the hand, the other against the back, moved the girls weightlessly in his arms. The beat pulsed through his body as he melted into the blur of swirling skirts and perfume.

The Crash of '29 jolted Sam back to reality. The Depression years saw his father and brothers without work. Two of his sisters found jobs to pay the bills for their family of nine. They owned a two-flat apartment house where they occupied the top floor. Rent from downstairs tenants covered taxes and upkeep. For Sam, the war couldn't have come at a better time. He enlisted immediately.

Codes of behavior established in his Chicago neighborhood had prepared Sam for life in the army. He earned his "stripes" in the trenches like he did in the streets, with his wits, hard work and loyalty. The men respected him, a respect that superior officers recognized by making him platoon sergeant. During the war's hot, muggy nights after exhausting troop marches to the front, Aragon memories sustained him. He longed to return home.

After the war ended, Sam returned to Chicago, to the ball-rooms, and to the unemployment lines. Dumb luck, he says, landed him a job as a printer's apprentice. Printing became his profession, as he gradually worked his way up to journeyman, typesetter, and night shift supervisor.

One Saturday night, like every other Saturday night for forty years, Sam hailed a cab to pick up Helen, his favorite dancing partner. Each had married others and raised their sons. There was no question of divorce; no question of disloyalty to their families; no question that they loved their arthritic spouses who had long since thrown away their dancing slippers. But for Sam and Helen, Saturday nights were theirs and theirs alone to dance.

Helen played ballroom music as she readied for their evening together. In slip and glittering blouse, she sat on the edge of the bed to put on her stockings. Strangely, a tingling dizziness came over her, so she eased back against the pillows to let it pass. Sam found her motionless body there. She had saved her last dance for him.

The ballrooms are dark now. The Aragon is closed and the big bands have disbanded one by one. But Sam and his friends dance on, every Saturday night at one small nightclub or another. Young gyrating couples stop briefly to watch the weightless "oldies" glide by. Then they turn to each other and touch, feel the music lift them slightly, ever so lightly off their feet, and move effortlessly into the night, like my father-in-law Sam, ninety-one years old and forever young.

Silver Carnations

You can't beat Eleanor. She's fourteen years old and has been in the family since 1989, when my husband bought her for me on Valentine's Day.

We had gone to an automobile dealership to look at a used stick-shift wagon for the kids' driving lessons and transportation. A test drive proved the wagon was a sluggish beast with barely enough oomph to handle a gentle slope, let alone the Ithaca hills in Upstate New York. We imagined our kids coasting backward into somebody's front yard while frantically searching for first gear. When we drove it back onto the lot, I spied a silver Volvo sedan, its boxy hulk tucked between two aerodynamic compacts.

"Why not take that one for a spin?" I suggested, the safety of our teenagers uppermost in my mind. I had read about the longevity and toughness of Volvos.

"We came here to buy a cheap clunker," Gordon sputtered in protest. "A standard shift student model, remember?"

Before I had a chance to answer, the salesman had ushered me behind the wheel, Gordon's question lingering in the air over the engine's purr. I sank appreciatively into the midnight blue upholstery. What a sweet buggy! Her road test was flawless.

Not yet convinced, Gordon arranged for an objective appraisal of the car by a local mechanic who specialized in servicing Volvos. The man could barely contain his enthusiasm. This particular model, the 240DL, he told us, had a simple, well-designed engine that we could reasonably expect to last for 250,000 miles! We signed on the dotted line that day.

"Such a survivor deserves a noble name," I thought. "How about Eleanor, in memory of Eleanor of Aquitaine and Eleanor Roosevelt? Yes, Eleanor fits."

We have extracted 192,000 of those promised miles from Eleanor, and she is just getting warmed up. After two teenagers and two collisions, she still doesn't have a scratch on her, but you should see the proverbial "other guy." Any driver who tangles with Eleanor ponders the wreckage of his pathetic junkheap and starts shopping for a "silver tank" of his own.

Everyone treats Eleanor with utmost respect. She has taken care of lots of human treasures, demanded little and given much. She earns her weekly shampoo and vacuum, biannual wax and polish, and regular tune-ups. In some households the family dog gets all the empty nesters' love and devotion. In ours, we cater to Eleanor.

She can't stop now. Before long the grandchildren will be clamoring for driving lessons.

Dandy Lions

One of the qualities that most attracted me to Gordon was his magnetism with children; they almost immediately sense his curiosity and fascination with them. He has the capacity to engage a child in conversation or play, even if only briefly, with a warm smile, a handshake and his full attention. His interactions with children are magical.

Children form unique relationships with nurturing adults. In the article "Discovering What Families Do," published in *Rebuilding the Nest* (Family Service America, 1990), Urie Bronfenbrenner, Professor Emeritus in Human Development at Cornell University, writes:

"In order to develop — intellectually, emotionally, socially, and morally — a child requires participation in progressively more complex reciprocal activity, on a regular basis over an extended period in the child's life, with one or more persons with whom the child develops a strong, mutual, irrational, emotional attachment and who is committed to the child's well-being and development, preferably for life."

Or, as Bronfenbrenner says more colloquially: "What is really needed to a ensure a happy, healthy and secure childhood is someone who is crazy about that kid."

Gordon is that kind of dad — a dad who is head-over-heels in love with his four children. We recently talked at length about the different dynamics that define his relationships with each of them: Terry and Cindy, daughters from his first marriage, and Geoff and Nikki, the son and daughter from ours.

"In the early years with Terry and Cindy, I was an absentee father," Gordon began. "I regret that. I was always out working or studying, holding jobs to support the family and go to school. My wife took care of the girls, as well as a few other children, to bring in household income." He and Jean divorced when Terry and Cindy were about five and seven years old.

After the divorce Gordon spent every other weekend with the girls. "I tried to counter the effects of divorce by keeping visits with Terry and Cindy regular and meaningful," he said. Their weekends together had a big effect on how his relationship with each of them developed from that time on. Frustrating to that development were the constant hellos and good-byes with long breaks in between.

Gordon and I met and began dating about two years after he divorced. My presence made weekends with Terry and Cindy more complicated emotionally. Terry was outwardly accepting of me but very quiet. Cindy still held out hopes that her parents would reconcile, so she begged me not to marry her father. I had fallen hard for Gordon, as both children could see. I was completely committed to making things work out for all four of us.

"I feel as though I did an injustice to Terry, my first-born," Gordon continued. "She was such a strong child, in charge and in control — a loner much like her dad. I mistakenly believed that she needed less of my help. She was the little mother to Cindy and very protective of her younger sister. Years later, when Terry finally confided in me about problems she had endured during her college years, I realized my mistake. She and I talk candidly now and have grown dramatically closer. She is a compassionate, loving and wonderful mother to her little boys. Having a family herself has brought us closer, too."

When Terry was a teen ager, she told me that she had tried to pretend I didn't exist, so that she wouldn't have to deal with having a stepmother. Her strongest loyalty was to her mother and appropriately so, I thought. She went through the motions of showing me affection but did not let herself develop a more personal relationship with me until after her mother remarried (about eight years after Gordon and I married).

Gordon described Cindy as an open, needy child from the very beginning, and she let him know that. "My role with Cindy has been to be empathetic, to be someone she can depend on emotionally. There is no particular incident I can point to, but Cindy has always been more overtly vulnerable and ready to look to me for help when she needs it."

Cindy and I have alternately clashed and bonded since the day we met. The emotional honesty between us has driven us apart at times but has also drawn us together. Stepparenting has been an exhausting challenge for me, and society in general offers little support. What I have always wanted is a loving connection with each of my stepdaughters that in no way challenges or threatens their primary bond to their mother. We have established that bond, but it has taken a long time, due to distance, time between visits and the births of Geoff and Nikki, among other things. Cindy responded immediately to the arrival of her new brother by moving in with us for a few weeks. She showered attention on him and also sought the reassurance she needed that her place in her dad's heart was still secure. In contrast, Terry held back and warmed to him slowly. They have both been caring big sisters.

"My relationship with Geoff unfolded within the context of athletics," Gordon said. "Through competition I wanted him to have the experience of putting out 100 percent effort, risking failure and overcoming fears of getting hurt. It was not so much the push to excel as the push to give his all in whatever he chose to do. Geoff's natural athleticism and interest in sports was a convenient vehicle for presenting challenges to him. I think competition is good for a child's development in general. I also wanted to offer Geoff something that you, as his mother, did not. You were the comforting, nurturing and sympathizing one. I chose to complement your role by challenging him to compete, to push the limits and to see failure as a worthwhile risk to take."

Geoff picked up his fear of getting hurt from me. I had seen many brawls at hockey games, caused by intentional high sticking and punching. One time, Geoff was checked into the boards from behind and knocked out cold. Gordon called it "getting his bell rung." I called it barbaric. Yes, Gordon did provide a role complementary to mine in the sports arena.

Athletics has been an important force in Gordon's life, as important to him as his academic degrees. "Athletics present young people with opportunities to discover what they are made of in ways few other experiences can," he told me. "On the field you're on the line."

Competing takes courage, sacrifice and risk; it demands consistent performance and often teamwork. Building athletic skills, like building skills in other spheres, tests one's character and contributes to feelings of self-worth, lessons that stay with children throughout their lives.

"Nikki defined our relationship very early on," Gordon continued. "I don't think she was even two years old when she openly disobeyed me, confidently and with a smile."

I remember that afternoon vividly. Nikki was standing on a chair, washing her baby dolls in the kitchen sink. Gordon decided that she had been splashing water everywhere long enough.

"Time to get down, Nikki," he said.

She turned and looked right at him and said, "No," then promptly turned back to the sink and continued splashing happily.

He sternly repeated the order. "Nicole, it's time to get down now."

She turned around again and said, "No."

At that point I had to leave the room to keep from bursting out laughing. I knew from experience that armchair directions rarely work with a two-year-old.

"Not accustomed to defiance, especially from a two-year-old,"

Gordon chuckled, "I had to grudgingly admire her independent spirit. I think that her stubborn streak and resistance to authority help to explain what we respect and admire in each other."

In Gordon's defense, he did walk over to the sink, lift Nikki down and show her how to mop the floor.

Competing takes courage, sacrifice and risk; it demands consistent performance and often teamwork. Building athletic skills, like building skills in other spheres, tests one's character and contributes to feelings of self-worth, lessons that stay with children throughout their lives.

"Children can survive and thrive in single parent families," Gordon concluded. "Having experienced fatherhood both ways, however, I am grateful for having been a full-time father with my second family. Fewer hellos and good-byes have meant a whole lot less making up for lost time."

Dwarf Trees

Of all the things I've ever lost, I miss my mind the most.
                                    — Anonymous.

Yesterday my hair turned gray. And my memory went South
for the winter. I swear I put my quilting pictures in a special envelope marked "quilts" and returned them to the picture box. Now I
can't find them anywhere. And the beaded necklace I always wear
with my red velour dress has disappeared from my jewelry case.
Last night when Gordon asked me what I was planning for dinner,
I couldn't remember the name of the vegetable — you know — the
green one that looks like little trees?

What is going on? Is this the early onset of Alzheimer's? No,
my friends say, it's only the beginning of turning fifty-something.
Of course my husband is delighted that I'm finally joining his crowd.
He tells me that nouns are the first to go. At sixty he's relieved he
still has all his adjectives and verbs. (That is something to be thankful for, I suppose.)

Up until yesterday I was too busy juggling to notice such
changes. You know the scene. Up at 6:00, make breakfast and bag
lunches for the kids, drop them off, head for work, rush through
appointments to leave time for taxiing kids to rehearsals or team
practices, rustle up dinner, help with homework, prepare for tomorrow, and collapse into bed. Who had time to notice midriff
bulge? Or the passage of twenty years? Or the first gray hair?

I guess I have always forgotten things occasionally, but I never
had much time to worry about it. Except the night I forgot to pick
Geoff up after practice and he hung around the field for an extra
hour, until I remembered and, with racing heart, flew over there,
imagining all the horrible things that could happen, and cried in
relief when I saw him at the edge of the field, in the dark, sitting on
his soccer ball ... I will never forget that.

Or the time we went to Nikki's eighth grade Christmas concert and after her chorus finished a couple songs, she walked over and picked up the microphone, and sang "Merry Christmas with Love," a solo that she had never told us about because she wanted it to be a surprise and, luckily, the video camera worked that night, as my heart stopped and tears of pride and joy filled my eyes ... I will never forget that either.

Then the kids left for college and our whirlwind schedule calmed to a breeze. We have more time for anything and everything now, including time to remember hundreds of life's unforgettable moments. What does it matter that I have lost the word "broccoli"?

Forget-Me-Nots

In our old neighborhood we looked for any excuse to hold a party. Sunny skies? Roll out the grills for a barbecue. Rain? Deal the cards. Vacation slides? Bring a dish-to-pass before the show. St. Paddy's Day? Serve up the green beer and corned beef sandwiches. The number one party instigator on our hill was Joe, vice president of a national corporation by day and host in orange sneakers by night. He and his wife Kay loved to throw parties. You name the occasion; they celebrated it.

Every New Year's eve they invented midnight games and re-lay races, like pass-the-grapefruit under your chin or the balloon between your knees. One year they set up a two-story miniature golf course throughout their rambling house. Kay cooked and served while Joe worked the crowd, telling hilarious stories one minute, listening attentively to each guest the next. He had a way of making people see life's possibilities — ever the optimist, never petty or mean-spirited.

All the kids in the neighborhood loved him, probably because he was a bit-o'-the-kid himself. One summer weekend Joe conspired with our son and his neighborhood pals to organize a picnic and kickball game in the empty lot next door. In the middle of the game, Joe backed down the driveway onto the pitcher's mound and popped the trunk. Inside were dozens of straw hats with striped hatbands for everyone, to add a touch of class to the festivities.

The week a German company bought out the corporation Joe worked for and downsized Joe out of a job, his employees stood around him crying. Who wanted to come to work without Joe around?

He landed on his feet, thankfully, by starting a family food brokerage business, which his son later owned and managed. Clients stood in line to buy merchandise from Joe because he always gave them more than they asked for, and he never let them down. He even managed to get boxcar loads of generic diapers into

Mexico, despite mountains of red tape. We know the diapers made it, but we're not sure what happened to the boxcars. Last we heard they were stranded somewhere in Northern Mexico. Oh, Joseph!

Kay kept the books and paid the bills for the business because Joe, ever the grand storyteller, tended toward exaggeration with numbers, too. "He never lies exactly," Kay winked. "He's just a bit reckless with the truth." She always gave him a blank check or two for emergencies, and he would tell her at week's end what he bought and how much he spent.

One month when Kay was reviewing the bank statement, she noticed that the figures Joe had given her didn't match the actual amounts — not even close. When she asked him about it, he apologized for his forgetfulness and promised to be more careful. But as the weeks went by, it was clear that his memory was playing tricks on him. In less than a year Alzheimer's and Parkinson's diseases began to take hold of our impish, garrulous friend.

The years passed and Joe gradually disappeared behind vacant eyes. Kay took total care of him. Their retirement plans hadn't included Alzheimer's, of course. Nor had their plans included Joe's panicky calls to the police because he couldn't find his wife, who happened to be napping upstairs. Nor did they include the day Joe forgot Kay's name. And nothing prepared Kay for the surges of rage she felt from exhaustion, frustration and the injustice of an illness that left her husband's body intact but stole his mind and spirit.

The time finally came when home care was impossible. Joe recognized no one and fell frequently, too weak and stiff to get up. After a few months of convalescent home care, he died, with Kay and his oldest daughter by his side. The family threw a party in his honor, just as Joe would have wanted. The occasion was too solemn for a rousing game of shoe golf with Joe's orange sneakers, so we reminisced about his humor instead.

We could almost hear Joe quip, "May you be in heaven a half

hour before the devil knows you're dead. And when you get there, look for me. I'm the one handing out the party hats."

Empire Apples

Now presenting, direct from the kitchen of our friends Ceil and Jim, a delicious recipe for Retirement Cake. Fix it anytime, because during retirement every day is a holiday!

Ingredients:

1 broom	3 wishes
3 chores	1 cup overflowing with imagination
1 mirror	1 newspaper
1 smile	dash of freedom

Take broom and sweep away fears of being a burden on friends and family. Replace concerns about loss of friends or identity with three short-term chores, such as transferring home movies onto videotape, painting a few rooms, or figuring out a workable budget on your retirement income.

Study your reflection in the mirror. Notice that you are still the same smart, talented and charming person. Brighten mirror image with the smile you reserve for your best friends. One delightful aspect of retirement is that you now have time to see them.

Remember that being old is a state of mind. Some fully employed people think and act old, long before their chronological age catches up.

Mix three wishes with cup of imagination and a dash of freedom. You are free to read, dance, travel, exercise, volunteer, play with your grandchildren, or take up new hobbies. Include both working and retired friends in your wishes. Some will be available weekdays; others on weekends. You are available anytime, so your circle of friends will grow. You are in demand!

One of Ceil and Jim's wishes is to live somewhere else for a time — maybe on a tropical island or, for big city excitement, on Manhattan Island. Since they grew up in New York City, they decide to cook up an urban getaway dish.

First, they select two mid-winter months close to the holidays, so they won't miss the spectacular decorations. Second, they scan the New York Times classifieds for furnished apartment sublets in midtown. (An essential ingredient is a second bedroom and bath for visitors.) Third, they arrange to visit affordable places with check in hand, ready to put down a security deposit when they find one that suits their tastes. Fourth, apartment secured, they relish planning their menu, as they sift through museum and theater listings and stir in visits from friends and family. Their grandchildren love the "Big Apple," as do Gordon and I.

Finally, preparations complete, the Manhattan Island feast begins. For Ceil, Jim and their guests, international entertainment and cuisine are just a stroll or cab ride away. Bon appetit!

Water Lilies

Last summer we drove to Cleveland to visit my stepdaughter, her husband and our two grandsons, ages two and four. A few blocks from their house we stopped off at a pet store to look for a surprise for the boys, something to contribute to the fun and memories of our few days together. We bought four little fish of different colors and a plastic bowl for them to swim around in.

The fish turned out to be the hit of the week, although I honestly don't know how they survived it. First the boys gave them names: Batman, Snuggles, Water Baby and The Pink Kisser. Then off we went to give the fish a tour of the backyard, where the boys picked up assorted leaves, twigs and stones to decorate the tank. They threw in a few ants and beetles for food.

By morning, the tank stank. Time to change the water. The boys had so much fun scooping water and fish from one container to another, they must have cleaned the bowl five or six times a day. The hardiest of the fish, by far, was The Pink Kisser, who literally jumped out of the scooping cup onto the back deck every time they tried to transfer him from one bucket to another. We rescued him repeatedly. Once he even flipped out of the cup, over the railing and off the deck, only to be returned to his pals unharmed and still swimming!

Water play is always a favorite activity with young children but the presence of little fish to take care of and watch stretched its popularity over many hours and days.

After we left for home, our son-in-law kept us informed about the fish, three of which died over the course of the next few months. I'm sure you can guess which one kept swimming strong. The Pink Kisser not only survived, but thrived, and grew to about four or five times its original size.

Our son-in-law bought a small aquarium with water filter and bubbler (so he wouldn't have to get out the garden hose every hour or so to change the water) and more little fish every now and then to keep The Pink Kisser company. The boys love to feed them, name them and make up stories about each one that they relate to us over the phone.

Last week when they called they were both chattering at once.

"Slow down, boys," Gordon said. "What happened?"

"Tiger (the cat) got The Pink Kisser in his mouth and was carrying him around in the kitchen," David said.

"Did he eat him?" I asked.

"No way. I grabbed the fish and put him back in the bowl," Dylan added proudly, "and he was still swimming!"

"But then he died," they both said.

"Aw, that's too bad, boys. He sure was a strong one, wasn't he?"

"Yeah, we're going to bury him in the backyard."

"You do a great job taking care of the fish, boys," I said. "The Pink Kisser was pretty special. We won't forget him, will we?"

It's the simple pleasures we remember the longest, don't you think?

Paperwhites

The notepad beside the telephone was perfect for pocket tales. Every day I rolled a sheet of 4" x 6" paper into an Underwood manual typewriter and pecked out simple mysteries. Each one featured different protagonists who encountered life-threatening crises just as I reached the bottom of the page. At that point I wrote, "Suddenly they all dropped dead. THE END."

I carefully folded each tale into a small square and stuffed them in my pockets to hand out to friends during recess. It never bothered them that all the characters dropped dead at the end. They were too busy talking about how they would rescue the hero from each predicament. My stories traveled from one classmate to the next, all around the playground. Naturally I kept writing new ones to keep my audience entertained and guessing.

I felt important when my friends gathered around to read the next pocket tale. Their interest inspired me to create ever more outrageous characters who faced tougher and tougher predicaments before they dropped dead. I especially wanted the boy who sat next to me to like me. After my pocket tales started circulating, he not only noticed me; he also passed me my very first love notes. At the end of that school year (I was in the fourth grade), I stopped story-writing and took up other pastimes.

Much later, during my year as a teaching intern, a shy third-grader named Liam began writing imaginative stories in response to a class assignment. I had asked each student to reach into a large paper bag full of ordinary objects, take one out and write a story from the point of view of that object. Liam drew a penny from the bag and wrote the first of many hilarious tales called "A Day in the Life of Benny the Penny." He wove robbers, unstitched pockets and overflowing rain gutters into his captivating stories. At the end of each tale the penny would get lost in some way — fall out of the hero's pocket or disappear down a storm drain — to be found by a new person (or animal) who became the hero in the next installment. Liam's classmates waited eagerly for every new Benny the Penny adventure, just like my classmates had waited for mine. Liam blossomed.

Marriage, motherhood, graduate school, professional pursuits and many other interests filled the intervening years. Although I wrote dozens of professional articles, I never wrote anything for publication until about five years ago.

My return to writing began with a gift. A friend gave me *The Artist's Way*, by Julia Cameron (J.P. Tarcher, 1992), a book that describes the creative process and many of the ways we inhibit ourselves from taking creative risks. The message rang true for me. Self-doubt or excuses have often prevented me from acting on my creative ideas.

I had thought about writing a book for children. The main character would be Granny Gumption, a salty old gal and a real problem-solver. No hand-wringing or bellyaching for her. Granny and I spent a few chapters together, but the story fizzled.

After that, I started writing about some of the experiences that have shaped my opinions and values. In the privacy of my journals, these became the basis for a series of opinion pieces. The decision to show them to someone else was the hardest step for me, a step that Cameron's advice helped me take.

"Once we admit the need for help, the help arrives," she writes. "The ego always wants to claim self-sufficiency. It would rather pose as a creative loner than ask for help. Ask anyway."

Asking for constructive but gentle criticism, I first approached Nikki, an excellent writer herself. I knew I could count on her to give honest reactions. Her thoughtful comments prompted some revisions, but most importantly, she genuinely liked my articles and we enjoyed the lively discussions they prompted.

Gordon and Geoff were my next in-house critics, helping me clarify sentences, improve word choices, and clean up my grammar. Little did I know they were such great cliché detectors and comma killers. They shot down my folksy dot-strings and hyphens, too.

Feeling much bolder, I sent five essays to the executive editor of our local newspaper, suggesting that he consider them as the first installments of a weekly column to be called, *Stand Up and Be Counted.* A week later, he accepted *Stand Up ...* for publication. I was overjoyed. Taking risks can reap rewards.

Since July 16, 1995, my weekly column has appeared in two more newspapers and is still going strong. I have branched out into editing and feature writing for magazines and Internet sites, too. My inner naysayers were wrong; perhaps yours are wrong, too.

Writing may not be your secret passion. You might long to sing professionally, dabble in photography, create films or dance on stage. Maybe a unique invention of yours will sell if you take the time to develop it and bring it to light. You are the only person who holds you back.

Chapter Seven
New Varieties

Human ingenuity knows no bounds. Fantasy can transport us through time and space onto imaginary planets, settled by aliens with superhuman powers. Wherever minds and imaginations lead us, we might actually follow. Who is to say how hybrids of our ancestors will live thousands of years from now? New life forms will continue to evolve on Earth and throughout the universe. You and I are planting the seeds.

Angel's Trumpet

Calling all kids! Calling all kids! Come here quickly and read this.

Does your town lack pizzazz? What is it like to live there? If you could do anything you want to change it, what would you do to make your neighborhood or town better?

Where I grew up, in Midland, Michigan, we lived on our bikes. Ten or fifteen of us were always outside, even when it rained, unless forked lightning flashed. There was a vacant lot next door and Barstow Woods was across the street, so we whiled away the hours making stick or snow forts and playing capture the flag, baseball, or "deer" (hide-and-seek played after dark with a flashlight). The neighbors especially liked the backyard carnival we threw every summer, complete with game booths, homemade prizes and wagon rides.

We could go anywhere in town on the bus for five cents. Sometimes we hopped on and rode the whole route, just for something to do. We could have gone downtown by bus, but there wasn't much to do there except shop. As I got older we stopped going there at all, because the new mall at the edge of town was more convenient. People called the main street a ghost town because of all the empty stores and boarded up windows there.

But you should see it now! A river flows behind the stores along Main Street. A second river intersects with it to form a "T" right behind the Farmer's Market. Someone designed and built a suspension "tridge" over the intersection of the two rivers. It is called a "tridge" because it has three spans that meet in the middle, right over the spot where the rivers meet. Built of dark wood and black cables, this unique structure captures the eyes of passersby, who are drawn closer to investigate. Only walkers, runners and bikers are allowed on it.

When I take my son and daughter to visit my hometown, they head for the "tridge" as fast as they can pedal. After spending time biking along the rivers, they buy fresh fruit at the Farmer's Market, where they can also rent canoes to paddle up and down the river. Developers, eager to capitalize on the rush of kids and families downtown, built a hotel and conference center, where businessmen and visitors can stay, rent bikes or canoes, stroll along the riverbanks, enjoy the outdoor sculpture garden on the opposite riverbank, and shop.

As the people came downtown, so did the merchants. There are clothing and toy stores, small restaurants and cafés, an art gallery, a drugstore, an arcade, a news and sundries shop, and a brand new hotel. More businesses are steadily moving in.

How do you suppose the citizens came up with the fanciful idea of a "tridge"? My guess is that it was invented by a child — or by a child at heart. Who else could dream up something so unique and playful, in such perfect harmony with the natural terrain?

That is why I am asking you, kids, to share your wonderful, whimsical ideas about improving your neighborhoods and towns. Talk with your friends or swap ideas with your parents. Many towns and neighborhoods could use imaginative ways to identify and celebrate their distinctive qualities.

Let your mind soar; then send your flights of fancy to the editor of your local newspaper. The mayor might listen and act on your ideas, too. A few new attractions could stop the ghosts from taking up residence on your streets!

Tomorrow's Yarrows

The computer has forever altered the world of information access and exchange. The other day I was watching a program on the Discovery Channel about technological advances that will be widely available within a few months. A man wearing a telephone headset was talking to his personal computer. When he spoke into the small microphone on his headset, the screen responded immediately to his commands.

He said the word "Yahoo" and the screen changed to show the Yahoo! search page. Any key word or sentence listed there came to the screen on command, without touching the keyboard. He spoke to the machine in a normal tone of voice in sentences, phrases, or single words. The next scene showed an Asian man doing the same thing; his machine responded equally accurately to commands in Japanese.

Voice-activated information lines already take calls to find tele-phone numbers and airplane flights. Physically handicapped people can control wheelchairs vocally. Soon the technology will be more widely available for home use. The day doesn't seem far off when keyboards will be unnecessary except for occasional changes or corrections in dictated text. One need only speak the message, name the punctuation, make spoken corrections and say, "Print." I'll be able to dictate stories while driving along in the car, play the tapes for my computer and receive a printed copy a few minutes later. Remarkable!

A technology expert we heard, who was speaking to a large audience, helped us imagine the next generation of telephones.

"When you hear the phone ring," he said, "you will put your thumb (input) to your ear and your little finger (output) to your lips, press a button on the battery pack around your waist and start talking!"

Input and output chips placed just under the skin of thumb and little finger create this newfangled phone.

From personal computer to VCR to TV to phone, soon we will surf the Internet for prime-time specials, interact with the cast from our sofas, and read or send e-mail on the screen during commercials. We can make phone calls from the couch, too, directly through the TV or, literally, on our fingertips. Why not? Put down the remote and tell the TV what you want. "Hello, Mushi Gardens? Chicken wings, pork-fried rice, and egg drop soup, for home delivery, please."

The whole technological revolution feels quite daunting, actually. The changes come along so rapidly, they make yesterday's breakthroughs today's white elephants. This fifty-something mind of mine can scarcely comprehend it.

People need time to assimilate change. When things happen so quickly, it seems as if they have not happened at all. A friend of mine put it this way: "Technology is a way of arranging the world so we don't have to experience it."

Maybe that is why so many people are deeply in debt. When we spend money by sliding a card through a slot or signing a piece of paper, it does not seem like real money, so the balance due at the end of the month hardly seems real either. I know what I will do. The next time I receive those bills in the mail, I will command the TV set to pay them!

Poison Sumac

It happened again yesterday. I was driving along the interstate behind a gleaming, black Lexus, when suddenly a cup flew out the window and tumbled to the side of the road. It was a Styrofoam cup — non-biodegradable and now a permanent blotch on the landscape.

Signs of such disregard for the environment abound. Contaminated ground water pollutes town wells; fish die mysteriously in lakes and streams; posted signs warn against swimming in scum-covered ponds. I never saw such signs as a child. When we swam near a waterfall, we thought nothing of opening our mouths under the spray for a refreshing drink. I would never do that today.

Recently, our household drinking water turned brown. When I called the water department about it, they told me they had been repairing a pipe under the street in our neighborhood, so we should expect some discoloration of the water for two or three days. Three weeks later we still had brown water. The next suggestion was that the muddy water caused by the repair efforts might have backed up into our hot water tank, causing the water to remain discolored longer than usual.

After another few weeks living with undrinkable water, we had a filter put on the water main coming into the house and re-placed the hot water tank. Success! For the time being anyway, we have clear, tasty water again.

I no longer take potable water for granted — nor does my friend Gail, who wrote to me last summer about a spoiled fishing outing with her sons.

"My two boys and I," she wrote, "hiked along a stream through the state park to a waterfall and watched the water tumble over the rocks to a wide basin below. Our attention was naturally drawn to the basin, to a dazzling fluorescent green covering that had col-lected in the calm area on the far side of the falls. What we noticed in this algae-like scum was trash — soda bottles, juice cartons and other man-made debris. We looked around for trash cans, but seeing none, walked farther along the stream to a shallow pool where we could see fish jumping for insects — a perfect spot for the boys to cast their fishing lines.

"I began a peaceful nap," Gail continued, "interrupted when the boys returned saying they no longer wanted to fish. Why? Because they had seen two young mothers come down to the water's edge, change their babies' diapers, roll up the soiled ones and push them between some stones in the stream! This foul sight brought our planned idyllic afternoon to a discouraging end."

How do we raise the awareness of every citizen to take responsibility for protection and preservation of our natural environment? We obviously need to do more.

As Chief Seattle, an influential Native American of the Suquamish tribe, reminded us in the mid-1850s:

"The rivers are our brothers. The air is precious, for all things share the same breath. This we know. The earth does not belong to man. Man belongs to the earth. All things are connected like the blood that unites one family. So if we sell you our land, love it as we have loved it. Care for it as we have cared for it. We may be brothers after all."

Individuals — young and old — and leaders of government and business must take the initiative to eliminate air and water pollutants, rather than responding grudgingly when threatened with fines, lawsuits or worse. Recognition of exemplary leaders who successfully reduce waste and pollution will challenge others to do the same. We need everyone's cooperation and participation to restore and preserve the spectacular natural beauty of our environment. Future generations are depending on us.

Sweet Rockets

Sit back and relax. Listen to your favorite music on the stereo and clear your mind of everyday clutter. Let me take you into a dream, into a place and time in the future when there will be a hover bubble in every garage.

Picture it with me. You are looking at a personal transport vehicle shaped like a large, flat-bottomed bubble. An array of sixteen cool-air jets covers the underside; the jets provide enough lift for the bubble to ride on a cushion of air about a foot off the ground. A magnetic force field surrounds each vehicle and acts as a protective shield to prevent it from colliding with anything. Drivers and passengers don't even have to watch where they are going!

The hover bubble runs on solar power with sufficient energy storage capacity to operate all night. Solar cells can also be recharged with electricity, available from any household outlet. Activated by voice or computer card, the occupant consults local maps and enters a destination into the onboard computer. The bubble then proceeds directly to that destination, over land or water because it needs neither roads nor flotation devices.

Hover bubbles come in different sizes to accommodate one or more people. They can be attached to each other simply by reversing the magnetic force field on one side of each bubble so they adhere together, thereby temporarily increasing the capacity for cargo or additional passengers.

Can you picture it yet? The solar-powered hover bubble creates no air pollutants, a relief for Mother Earth's ailing atmosphere. Safe enough for a child to "drive," children will have their own bubbles with adult-programmed destinations installed. (Pre-programming prevents kids from taking off for Florida during recess.) Children's bubbles come equipped with special tracking devices, so parents always know where their children are. Kids can travel readily to and from school, daycare, friends' houses or the mall.

The hover bubble will change the world even more than the telephone, computer, car or Hula-Hoop did. Now all we need, fellow dreamers, is an engineer to draw us a picture or, better yet, build us a prototype.

Just imagine. A few years from now, you are relaxing in your favorite easy chair, your mind adrift and dreaming, when out of the corner of your eye you notice something float by the window. As you watch, astonished, it glides across the yard and slides into your garage. You smile knowingly, remembering the hover bubble story; then you stretch back in the recliner to imagine some future time when one of your inventions becomes a reality.

Olive Branches

Strong gusts of wind whipped dust and bits of paper across the sidewalk. I drew my scarf protectively over my face and tried to hold the bottom of my coat closed against the knee-numbing cold. I was so intent on rushing across the park to the subway station, I nearly tripped and fell over two men who lay on the ground, their bodies curled together for warmth.

"Bums," I thought in disgust, as I hurried on. But I could not get the picture of them out of my mind. Emaciated bodies in frayed wool coats. Empty liquor bottles strewn at their feet. Faded jeans, matted hair and unshaven faces. People at a dead end.

My conscience began to nag at me. "Maybe I should try to find a policeman," I thought. "No, he would arrest them for loitering and throw them in jail for the night. At least they'd get a meal and some protection from the elements. Only to return to the streets the next day. That's no solution."

Relieved to reach the warm station, I bought tokens, caught the next train uptown, and settled in to read the morning paper. But the headlines kept blurring before my eyes, as images of the inert men forced their way into my mind. I wondered if they had wives or children. Neither of them looked much over forty. What had happened to derail their lives? How many more dispossessed people fill the dark corners of abandoned buildings or huddle under bridges at night on their way to nowhere?

"Maybe there's a shelter nearby," I thought. "The staff there could counsel the men and help them find them work. The cost of providing them with food, clothing and shelter represents a tiny fraction of our national wealth. But are free handouts an answer? Yes, at least until they get back on their feet."

Still, I did nothing.

My thoughts and feelings about the homeless run the gamut

from hostility to compassion to curiosity to indifference to fear. No one is immune from desperation. I have heard that the largest-growing poverty group in America is single mothers and their children. Surely poverty is never a part of any mother's plans.

Some weeks later, I read an article in the February 1998 issue of *US Airways Magazine* about breaking the homeless cycle. Secretary Andrew Cuomo of the Department of Housing and Urban Development said, "In many ways, the word 'homeless' is a misnomer. Not having a home is but one aspect of a continuum of concerns that must be addressed for most homeless persons to reach self-sufficiency."

The homeless need more than food, shelter, and clothing; they also need transitional housing, daycare, parenting education, medical care, job skills, job placement services and mentoring. Federal and state governments have increased funding to agencies that provide a continuum of care for the homeless. Cuomo created a national hotline that anyone can call to find assistance for a homeless person. The number is 800-483-1010. As of January 2001, this referral service was still active. State departments of social services can also provide referrals to people who wish to volunteer their time to help those in need.

I rarely put coins in a beggar's cup. Nor do I invite the homeless to reside with me. I can and do, however, contribute money, clothing or food to the homeless shelter nearest me; and I can and will carry the national hotline number in my wallet, so the next time I see or meet someone so unprotected I can make a phone call. Were I in his or her shoes, I hope someone would do the same for me.

Solomon's Seal

Americans find live courtroom drama riveting, because they want to see justice served. During the O.J. Simpson trial, however, the entire nation learned that justice has many faces. Evidence does not speak for itself. The nature of its message changes through the eyes of each beholder, be he judge, attorney, defendant, juror or witness. The same evidence can even produce opposite verdicts, as we saw in the Simpson criminal (not guilty) vs. civil (guilty) proceedings.

Under the glare of TV cameras the justice system goes on trial, too. It reassures us to witness careful jury selection, painstaking preparation by attorneys, attention to minute details of evidence and testimony — all under the direction of an impartial judge. Why? Because we want such diligence for ourselves, if we ever need it. We believe in the fundamental premise of our justice system: that each man and woman who stands accused of a crime is innocent until proven guilty.

But what happens in court away from the cameras? Does our legal system generally treat people fairly? How do factors other than basic fairness and the rule of law affect the court's decisions? Consider the following situations.

Angela rushed a national sorority during her freshman year in college. As part of initiation she and two other new members were sent on a scavenger hunt. One of the items on their list was a toilet paper dispenser, which they collected by ripping it off a bathroom stall wall. They were caught red-handed and arrested for vandalism.

The judge decided to treat them harshly as a deterrent to other fraternity/sorority excesses and sentenced them to three days in jail. Parental persuasion, character references and absence of prior arrests made no difference to the judge. Upon her release, Angela, in utter humiliation, dropped out of school. Was justice served in this case?

In a second case, Vincent, a graduate student from Caracas, struggled to make ends meet. He worked nights as a busboy in a small restaurant and convinced himself that he deserved the food and dishes he sometimes took home after work. Petty thievery escalated to shoplifting and stealing cash or clothing from student dormitory rooms. Students reported their losses to campus police, who conducted interviews and lie detector tests of several students, including Vincent. They also planted a decoy wallet covered with an invisible powder to pick up fingerprints, which later proved to be Vincent's.

But no arrest or restitution of property occurred. To avoid embarrassment and international ill will (from Vincent's prominent Venezuelan family) university officials quietly arranged for Vincent to leave the country. Was justice served in this case?

Recently, issues of fairness were publicly scrutinized during the hotly contested presidential election of 2000 – a story that may never fully be told.

Throughout our lives we learn to settle conflicts at every level of society — at home, on the playground, at school, in business and in government. Our courts are the final arbiters of justice. Principles of fairness and the rule of law must prevail over political influence, money, power, persuasion, legal loopholes or judicial whim. Otherwise our laws are no more than a mirage, visible on the books but invisible in court.

Star Magnolia

Eight-year-old Nikki and I looked forward to the spring planting season. Each year we tilled the soil and raked it smooth before settling into our hypnotic routine. Dig the furrows, place the seeds, cover them gently, dig the furrows, place the seeds, cover them gently. Conversation flowed easily between us, nourishment for fertile minds.

"Mom, has there ever been a woman president?"

"No, there hasn't, honey," I answered. "Women have led other countries but never the United States."

"Why?"

"Maybe no American woman has ever wanted the job badly enough," I speculated. "Our society discourages women from striving for positions of power and authority."

The seeds took root in Victoria Woodhull soil.

In 1872, Woodhull, a stockbroker and publisher, was the first woman to run for president of the United States. A candidate of the Equal Rights Party, she fought for women's social and political rights. Her candidacy became embroiled in controversy. Unfortunately her name never appeared on the ballot because she was only 34 years old, a year under the constitutionally mandated age of 35.

"Could I become president?" Nikki wanted to know.

"Certainly you could," I replied. "You have the talent and intelligence to be whatever you want to be. With careful planning and hard work you can achieve any goal you set for yourself."

Belva Lockwood raindrops nourished the tender seedlings under sun-drenched skies.

In 1884, Lockwood, the first woman attorney admitted to argue before the Supreme Court, was the next woman presidential candidate, also on the Equal Rights Party ticket. She received more than four thousand votes from six states and was nearly awarded Indiana's electoral votes.

Dig the furrows, place the seeds, cover them gently.

"Some of my friends are letting their grades slide, Mom. They won't make decisions without talking to their boyfriends first. Do I have to do that, too?"

"No, Nikki, you don't have to compromise your academic or social standards for anyone. Your friends will admire you for being true to yourself."

The saplings drew strength from Margaret Chase Smith winds.

Not until 1964, eighty years after Lockwood's effort, did another woman seek the presidency. Smith, Republican senator from Maine, served in both houses of Congress for a total of thirty years. A voice of conscience against political witch-hunts, she campaigned in New Hampshire, Illinois and Oregon primaries, but her name was not placed in nomination.

Nikki presided over Key Club and the mock legislative senate in high school. She excelled academically and graduated first in her class.

"Love life, spread positive energy and create stable families," she advised classmates in her valedictory speech. "Thanks to our families and friends, teachers and guidance counselors for helping us learn, love and achieve our goals."

Shirley Chisholm sunlight warmed the quiescent buds, which burst into bloom.

Chisholm, the first African-American woman ever elected to

Congress, ran for president in 1972. In favor of all-volunteer armed forces, nondiscriminatory hiring practices, and guaranteed annual income for the poor, she entered primaries in twelve states. She won twenty eight delegates and received 152 first-ballot votes at the Democratic National Convention.

"I never want to leave this place," Nikki sighed, gazing out the arched dormitory window. "I feel like I belong here."

And so she did. All the planning and hard work won her admission to Princeton, a place where dreams take wing.

Geraldine Ferraro bees pollinated the blossoms.

Ferraro received great recognition and public scrutiny when she accepted the Democratic nomination for vice president in 1984. A three-term congresswoman from New York, she had won wide public attention as head of the Democratic Party's platform committee. The Mondale-Ferraro ticket was defeated.

"My boyfriend and I had a big argument last night, Mom. I think he finally understands that my future goals are as important as his are. I want him to celebrate my ambitions, not squelch them."

"Keep talking and listening, Nikki," I advised. "You can learn how to create true partnerships with others."

Petals blanketed the ground in the glow of Patricia Schroeder stars.

Schroeder made a bid for the White House in 1988, only to drop out of the primaries because she could not raise enough money to mount a national campaign. As a longstanding and influential member of Congress, she had the credentials to compete for the presidency, but lacked the power base to gain the nomination.

Dig the furrows, place the seeds, cover them gently.

"Still no woman at the top, Mom."

"You can go there," I said. "Or another woman can. Someone has to go first."

"I know, Mom. I can be whatever I want to be."

When the trees bear fruit on Inauguration Day, daughters throughout the world will reap the harvest.

Rose of Cotton

Patches of calico fill the quilter's palette with hues and prints of soft cotton, ready to record history and dreams in cloth. Chronicles of our lives are as important to us as living them. We sing, dance, write and weave — make pottery, movies, paintings and artifacts — so that others might know and remember us. Many years ago I was drawn to making quilts to commemorate events and people in my life.

We lived high on a hill then, on a cul-de-sac in the middle of town. Ours became a close knit neighborhood quickly, thanks to the blizzard of '78, which dumped so many feet of snow on Massachusetts that the state shut down for a week. Eventually the plows made their way to our hilltop, but not before we had shoveled each other out and spent many hours playing bridge and concocting odd meals from the shared foodstuffs in our kitchens.

While drinking hot tea across the street at Gloria's house, I admired the breathtaking quilts that hung on the entryway and living room walls. She had designed and made them herself, she told me, using brilliant splashes of color in bold Scandinavian designs. As we pored over several quilting books together, I especially liked the classic symmetry of Colonial patterns like the log cabin, cherry baskets and flying geese. Gloria agreed to teach me how to make one.

"What a wonderful gift for Dad's upcoming retirement," I thought. I chose the bear's paw design for his quilt, rendered in deep masculine colors of gold, black, blue and maroon in plain and paisley cottons. Each step in the process appealed to me, from the meticulous cutting and piecing, to assembling the layers, to hand-sewing the layers together in curvilinear swirls of tiny stitches. The individual paw print blocks, when pieced together, created larger designs in the interplay of light and dark shapes. For an added personal touch, I stitched a message into the lining.

Making quilts appeals to me, I think, because so much of what

I do as a mental health professional produces no visible product. I can sense the progress individuals make in the process of counseling, but I cannot always see it. So having something tangible to hold and admire after so many months of work is tremendously satisfying. And quilting puts me in touch with the eternal flow of our hearts and minds through time.

I have made five more quilts since finishing Dad's, each one a celebration of a special person or event. A log cabin pattern in joyful, lavender prints for my daughter; plaid stars with silver threads for my son; schoolhouses surrounded by silhouettes of children holding hands to mark the birth of my first grandson; soaring eagles of peace for my husband; and a midnight garden of tulips and buttercups to capture the essence of spring, a time of renewal and hope. Quilt patterns for my stepdaughter's inquisitive toddlers are just beginning to take shape in my mind.

Our family's like a patchwork quilt,
With kindness gently sewn.
Each piece is an original
With beauty of its own.
With threads of warmth and happiness
It's tightly stitched together,
To last in love throughout the years ...
Our family is forever.
                              — Author Unknown

Appendix
Roots

The Internet is fertile ground for learning about human development. Web sites listed on the following pages are ripe with information about the topics introduced in *Wild Tulips*.

Roots

Chapter One: Seedlings

Plenty of Thyme
Influence of grandparents on grandchildren:
http://ndsuext.nodak.edu/extpubs/yf/famsci/ fs548w.htm
1900 vs. now: *http://www.time.com/time/ time100/timewarp/timewarp.html*

Braidwood Brilliant
Inventors and Inventions: *http://www.150.si.edu/150trav/ remember/amerinv.htm*
Genius: *http://www.centrum.is/nucleus/iq.property.html*
Gifted resources home page: *http://www.eskimo.com/ ~user/kids.html*

Scent of Jasmine
Disciplining children:
http://www.childparenting.about.com/parenting/ childparenting/cs/discipline/
Taking children seriously: http://*www.eeng.dcu.ie/~tcs/ Journal/tcsjournal.html*

Monk's Beard
Abbey at Gethsemane: *http://www.monks.org/*
"Call" or choice: *http://acad.smumn.edu/merton/ call%26choice.html*

Mock Orange
Placebo Effect: *http://altmed.od.nih.gov/oam/cam/1997/ jan/2.htm*
Alternative remedies: *http://www.holisticmed.com/*

Black-Eyed Susans
Adaptive technology helps blind and visually impaired:
http://newsline.byu.edu/newsline/Archives/news/ 9702/970221VISION3.HTM

Hand in Hand: materials to use with disabled: *http://
www.afb.org/c_multi.html*

Passion Blossoms

Measure your EQ (Emotional Quotient): *http://
www.utne.com/cgi-bin/eq-*

Emotional Intelligence
*http://trochim.human.cornell.edu/gallery/young/
emotion/htm*

Cupid's Dart

Courtship corner: http://www.talkcity.com/courtship/

Long-distance romance: http://www.cyber-loving.com/

Chapter Two: Nutrients

Chatterboxes

Infant brain development: *http://members.aol.com/
WStaso/gbprs.htm*

Newborns: Growth and development:
*http://www.kidsource.com/kidsource/pages/
newborns.growth.html*

Baby's Breath

Quality childcare choices: *http://www.carnegie.org/
starting_points/startpt3.html*

Tips for teen babysitters: *http://www.ncpc.org/10yth1.htm*

Silent Verbena

Body Language: *http://www.angelfire.com/co/
bodylanguage/page6.html*

Subliminal messages:
*http://www2.4anything.com/search?q=
Subliminal+Messages&cpg=%3B028039a*

Mistletoe

Family giving tree: *http://www.FamilyGivingTree.org/*

Mistletoe lore:
*http://www.ag.usask.ca/cofa/departments/hort/
hortinfo/misc/ mistleto.html*

Mums and Poppies
Raising Parents: *http://www2.itexas.net/~BillPen/ Child23.htm*

Kids speak out: *http://www.child.net/kidspeak.htm*

Mountain Laurel
Inner limits of mankind: *http://www.jyu.fi/~rakahu/ erwin.html*

Build self-esteem:
http://www.interactiveparent.com/family/growth/ self-esteem.htm

Lonely Petunia
Selective Mutism:
http://personal.mia.bellsouth.net/mia/g/a/garden/ garden/index.htm

Attachment Disorders: *http://www.cuddletime.com/ attach1b.html*

Dash of Sage
Health issues among teens:
http://www.enconnect.net/ujw/1996/yousa/ mindex.htm

Parenting today's teen: *http://www.parentingteens.com/ editor.html*

Hidden Truffles
Anxiety: *http://anxiety.cmhc.com/*

Value of psychotherapy: *http://www.ccemhc.org/ 16value.html*

Chapter Three: Growth

Indian Paintbrush
Rules of discipline: *http://www.parentsoup.com/experts/ el_discipline.html*

Parenting:*http://babyparenting.miningco.com/ msubguide.htm*

Late Bloomers

Learning styles: *http://members.aol.com/susans29/lsa.html*

Marching to different drummers: *http://www.ascd.org/readingroom/books/guild98book.html*

Wild Tulips

The power of language: *http://www.mtoomey.com/poweroflanguage.html*

Character education resources: *http://www.indiana.edu/~eric_rec/ieo/bibs/characte.html*

Larkspurs

Nationwide community service opportunities: *http://entp.hud.gov/volunter.html*

Motivating the unmotivated student: *http://www.ed.gov/databases/ERIC_Digests/ed370200.html*

C-c-crocuses

Stuttering:*http://www.wiu.edu/users/mfrwq/stuthome.html*

Speech and language development: *http://ws1.kidsource.com/ASHA/*

Causes of stuttering: *http://www.mankato.msus.edu/dept/comdis/kuster/Kehoe/FAQstuttering.html*

Colt's Foot

Charlie's Sneaker Pages: *http://sneakers.pair.com/index.htm*

Teach kids about money: *http://www.familyeducation.com/article/0,1120,37-6106,00.html*

School Daisies

First day of school:
http://www.mdausa.org/publications/Quest/
q44first.html

What is a school psychologist?
http://www.bartow.k12.ga.us/psych/psych.html

Variegated Ivy

Get into any college: *http://www.101online.com/*
welcome.html

Starting points for college-bound students: *http://*
www.ets.org/spstud.html

Climbing Wisteria

Glass Ceiling: *http://cyberwerks.com:70/1s/dataline*

Top 100 companies for women: *http://*
www.womweb.com/100intro.htm

Chapter Four: Pests

Beetle Balm

World War II: *http://www.pbs.org/greatwar/interviews/*
massie5.html

Think Sideways: Essays about tribalism, racism, sexism
and stereotyping:
http://www.orbonline.net/~think/sideways/
index.html#SOCIAL

Flame Bushes

Fire safety: *http://www.aurorafire.gov/quiz3.htm*

Prevention: *http://firestation24.com/index.htm*

Bleeding Hearts

Near-death studies: *http://www.indra.com/iands/*
index.html

New York migrant education: *http://*
snyoneab.oneonta.edu/~thomasrl/

Stinging Nettles

Spanking: *http://www.angelfire.com/on3/todayschild/spanking.htm*

Promoting self-control in children: *http://nrc.uchsc.edu/kansas/ka_3_035.htm*

Shooflies

Developmental milestones (birth to three): *http://www.liidp.org/growth_milestones.html*

Early Childhood Care and Development: *http://www.ecdgroup.com/eccd.html*

Perennial Flax

Privacy in america: is your private life in the public eye? *http://www.netstoreusa.com/ljbooks/025/0252016041.shtml*

Politics and family life: *http://www.bookstore.com/lieberman.html*

On becoming a school leader: *http://www.ascd.org/readingroom/books/combs99book.html*

Swamp Grass

Environmental hazards in the home: *http://www.envirohome.com/index.html-ssi*

Toxins and pollution: *http://www.haribon.org.ph/toxins.htm*

Shepherd's Purse

Debt:*http://www.troubleshooter.com/columns/CREDIT_CARD_DEBT.html*

Reestablish credit: *http://www.consumercredit.com/*

Lamb's Ears

Children and TV violence: *http://www.psych.med.umich.edu/web/aacap/factsfam/violence.htm*

Youth radio: *http://www.youthradio.org/text/viewsTxt/culture/TV.html*

Chapter Five: Harvest

Bean Sprouts

Kids' fascination with seeds and dirt: *http://www.kidsgardening.com/*

Little Sprouts — Gardening and your kids: *http://www.dlcwest.com/~createdforyou/sprouts.html*

Kids' gardening sites: *http://www.yourperfectlandscape.com/Klinks.html*

Sunflowers

Boyhood to manhood: *http://www.menstuff.org/books/byissue/therapy-general.html*

College costs: *http://www.ets.org/fpoints/*

Pumpkin Seeds

Stepparents: *http://www.ag.ohio-state.edu/~ohioline/hyg-fact/5000/5231.html*

Blended Families: *http://www.ca-probate.com/a_blendd.htm*

Chat room for families: *http://drizzle.com/families.html*

Morning Glories

Incorporating music into the school day: *http://home.att.net/~mikejaqua/news/march-April-00.html*

Music and the developing brain: *http://parenting-baby.com/Parenting-Baby-Music-Research/Music-Research.html*

Shrinking Violets

Anorexia Nervosa and Other Eating Disorders (ANRED): *http://www.anred.com/*

Body image and young girls: *http://www.research.umbc.edu/~korenman/wmst/bodyimage.html*

Grape Vines

The Children of Separation and Divorce Center: *http:// cosd.bayside.net/*

Fathers for Justice: *http://www.ffj.on.ca/*

The Friendship Page: *http://www.ozemail.com.au/ ~polsonhr/*

Marigolds

Seven Secrets for a Successful Marriage: *http://www.lifehelp.org/lifeissues/cli26.htm*

International couples: *http://www.geocities.com/Heart land/4448/Couples.html*

Beach Plums

10 Best family vacations: *http://www.travelling- magazine.com/articles/family.cfm*

Family reunion planning: *http://www.family-reunion.com/*

Great Lakes Commission: *http://www.glc.org/*

Snapdragon Puppets

Phenomenon of recovered memory: *http://www.vuw.ac.nz/psyc/fitzMemory/ contents.html*

Intergenerational learning: *http://www.temple.edu/CIL/ what.html*

Chapter Six: Regeneration

Creeping Buttercups

Weight Loss for Seniors: *http://weightloss.about.com/health/weightloss/ msubseniors.htm?iam=mt*

Management: *http://www.realtime.net/anr/weightmg.html*

Lady Slippers

History of the Aragon ballroom and other great Chicago dancehalls: *http://www.suba.com/~scottn/explore/ sites/ballroom/ballroom.htm*

Learn ballroom dance steps: *http://www.dancetv.com*

Silver Carnations

Teen driving pledge plus related links: *http:// www.teendrivingpledge.com/*

Volvo Club of America: *http://www.vcoa.org/irv-o-meter.html*

Crash test data: *http://www.nhtsa.dot.gov/cars/testing/ ncap/*

Dandy Lions

Fathering Magazine: *http://www.fathermag.com/*

National Center for Fathering: *http://www.fathers.com*

Dwarf Trees

Memory enhancement: *http://www.demon.co.uk/ mindtool/memory.html*

Normal forgetfulness: *http://www.msnbc.com/news/ 375727.asp*

Forget-Me-Nots

Alzheimer's: *http://www.alzheimers.com/*

Neighborhoods: *http://www.sc.edu/ifis/naf.htm*

Empire Apples

Retirement planning: *http://www.fool.com/Retirement/ Retirement.htm*

Elderhostel: *http://www.elderhostel.org/*

Water Lilies

Grand-loving with activities and long distance fun: *http://world.std.com/~jcarlson/senior/*

Grandparenting: *http://www.seniors-site.com/grandpar/*

Paperwhites

Making a career change: *http://www.ivillage.com/content/categories/ 0,1825,1909~48,00.html*

Creativity at work: *http://www.creativityatwork.com/ links.htm*

Mid-life career choices: *http://www.usnews.com/usnews/edu/beyond/ grad/gblate.htm*

Chapter Seven: New Varieties

Angel's Trumpet
> Ghost towns of America: *http://www.ghosttowns.com/*
> City of the future: *http://www.tripeast.com/futntr.htm*

Tomorrow's Yarrows
> Voice activated machines: *http://www.automatedliving.com/*
> Future technologies: *http://bce.ca/bce/e/magazine/world/view/*
> Cyberchip implant: *http://www.cnn.com/TECH/computing/9808/28/armchip.idg/*

Poison Sumac
> Discussion of Chief Seattle's speech of 1854: *http://www.thehistorynet.com/WildWest/articles/02965_text.htm*
> Earth Day: *http://www.cfe.cornell.edu/EarthDay/ednethome.html*
> Environment/Recycling Hot Line: *http://www.1800cleanup.org/text/main.htm*

Sweet Rockets
> Descriptions and drawings of commercially available hovercraft: *http://www.hoverwork.co.uk/index1.html*
> Patenting inventions: *http://www.mannpa.com/faq.html*

Olive Branches
> Shelter Issues in U.S.: *http://www.shelter.org.uk/issues.html*
> CT services for the homeless: *http://www2.ari.net/nch/local/connecticut.html*

Solomon's Seal
> Media bias with courtroom cameras: *http://www.cnn.com/US/9611/25/simpson.sidebar/*

Innocent until proven guilty:
http://www.daily.iastate.edu/volumes/Fall95/
95se21/edit2.html

Star Magnolia

First woman to run for president: *http://www.victoria-*
woodhull.com/

American Women Presidents: *http://*
www.americanwomenpresidents.org/

Rose of Cotton

Quilting in the 1930's: *http://www.cranstonvillage.com/*
quilt/q-1930s.htm

Earthly immortality: *http://www.lib.muohio.edu/~mlh/*
summary.html